IAMREDEMP†ION

IAMREDEMP✝ION

Catching God's heart

Andy Elmes

Copyright © 2014 Andy Elmes

Published in 2014 by Great Big Life Publishing
Empower Centre, 83-87 Kingston Road, Portsmouth, PO2 7DX, UK

The right of Andy Elmes to be identified as the author of this work has been asserted by
him in accordance with the Copyright, Designs and Patents Act 1988.

British Library Cataloguing in Publication Data.

A catalogue record for this book is available from the British Library.

ISBN-13: 978-0-9928027-4-5
ISBN-10: 0992802741
EBOOK: 978-0-9928027-5-2

Unless otherwise marked, Scripture quotations are taken from The Holy Bible, New
King James Version. Copyright © 1979, 1980, 1982 by Thomas Nelson, Inc. Used by
permission. All rights reserved.

Scripture quotations marked 'NASB' are taken from the New American Standard Bible.
Copyright © 1960,1962,1963,1968,1971,1972,1973,1975,1977,1995 by The Lockman
Foundation. Used by permission.

Scripture quotations marked 'NIV' are taken from The Holy Bible, New International
Version (Anglicised edition). Copyright © 1979, 1984, 2011 by Biblica (formerly
International Bible Society). Used by permission of Hodder & Stoughton Publishers, an
Hachette UK company. All rights reserved.

Scripture quotations marked 'The Message' are taken from The Message. Copyright © 1993,
1994, 1995, 1996, 2000, 2001, 2002. Used by permission of NavPress Publishing Group.

Contents

DEDICATION

To my dear friends Phillip and Chrissie Cameron and all at Stella's Voice.

I would like to dedicate this book to you. Your ministry sums up and personifies the very heartbeat I have tried to capture within the pages of this book. My life was radically impacted when I met you and your precious family. You caused me to understand the power of redemptive love in a way I never could have imagined. Relentlessly you spend your lives for the redemption of those forgotten and abandoned by others. Witnessing their lives restored is one of the most beautiful things I have ever seen. Keep on doing what you do – it's amazing!

We love you and stand with you,

Andy and Gina (and the tribe)

Phillip and his family run a truly incredible ministry called Stella's Voice, which is working with both the orphans of Moldova and young girls who are victims of trafficking. The work of Stella's Voice is truly amazing, and it would not be right for me to write a book on the power of redemptive love without mentioning this man and this ministry. Please take a moment to visit their website. If you are looking for inspiration concerning the power of radically changed lives, they will blow your mind and stir your heart. You, too, can become Stella's Voice.

www.stellasvoice.org

Who is Andy Elmes?

A ndy Elmes is a pastor, leader, published author and popular conference speaker. He and his wife Gina lead Family Church, a multi-congregational church consisting of several church plants located primarily around the South of England, as well as two congregations in the Philippines.

Andy is a strategist who thinks outside of the box, very much the visionary, never short of a new way forward. He heads up a number of other ministries including **Synergy Alliance**, **Synergy Christian Churches** and **Great Big Life**. Each of these seeks to empower and equip leaders and people to live the biggest life they can.

He has authored a number of books, as well as having a globally-read internet devotional called *Breakfast of Champions*. He is always in great demand as a conference speaker and is known for speaking in a life-filled and very animated way, bringing God's truth in a way you'll never forget. Andy's heart beats as that of an evangelist, and he loves to see the lost won to Christ and the Church mobilised and equipped to do so. Over the years he has become a pastor to many other pastors, walking with them and standing by them as they live out the dream God has given them. From over twenty fruitful years in ministry, planting churches and leading leaders, he brings great wisdom and a Christ-centred focus to those he pastors and works with.

Andy and Gina have five lovely children – Olivia, Ethan, Gaby, Sophie and Christina – and are committed to seeing each of them grow to love God, know his ways and discover all that God has for them. They reside in Portsmouth, UK.

INTRODUCTION

IAMREDEMPTION is not just a book – it's a mandate, a challenge, a clarion call for the people of God to understand afresh the power of redemption; to be mobilised to tell others of their story of redemption; and to be a carrier of redemption to the lives of others. In this book, you will read about the moment when the redemptive heart of God came into my world and turned it upside down. Instantly I understood God's love for humanity like never before, realising afresh that the desire of His heart is still that none would perish. The question is, what are we prepared to do about that desire?

Redemption purchased humanity back to God and His design for them, but it is a much richer word than that. Redemption is also the power of God in a person's everyday life to make fresh and alive again things that have died. It is to give hope where hopelessness has reigned for far too long, to heal the sick, and restore the broken. Redemption is the very heart of God for the humanity He never stopped loving. Jesus put it so well when he said, *'Behold, I make all things new.'* This is redemption.

Today our God looks for those who will catch His redemptive heart and then carry it into the needy worlds of others, who will grasp the truth that His heart still breaks for the broken and His hand still reaches out to the needy. Can you feel a stirring? While so much of His church sits comfortably and sings nice songs to Him week in and week out, an army is stirring and rising to its feet. An army that wears no uniform, that has no rank. Just hearts marked with a common godly heartbeat, an army of everyday people wearing everyday clothes, who have a passion to take the redemptive heart of God into their everyday worlds.

How about you? Will you sit quietly while a world cries help? Will you cross the road when you encounter need or will you be like the Good Samaritan and walk head first towards theneedsofothers?WiththebattlecryofIAMREDEMPTION, believing God can and will use your life to change the storyline of others for His glory and fame!

An alarm clock is going off; we cannot stay quiet anymore about the incredible things He has done in our lives. We cannot remain 'asleep in the light' when there remains around each of us such a great ocean of need. Let us awaken, arise and purpose to live beyond ourselves as He lived beyond Himself for us. To lay down the luxuries of things like comfort and preference, to be the army He needs us to be. An army that is marked with the simple conviction of IAMREDEMPTION! I have received it and I will now be a carrier of it in the lives of others.

Are you ready to be challenged? Are you ready to be dangerously provoked? Are you ready for Christianity to get exciting again? Then read on . . .

IAMREDEMP✝ION.org STORIES

Broken teenager, restored

I came to know God as a young teenager after my dad had persuaded me to come to church. I had grown up too fast and tried things you shouldn't have at my age! I smoked, drank, taken drugs, and was dating people way above my own age. I was severely depressed and, after a particular drinking session, I was rushed to hospital and resuscitated. After that moment in my life I began cutting myself and having suicidal thoughts.

So when my dad continued to pester me I decided there was nothing to lose in coming to church. The day I walked into Family Church I felt like a weight had been lifted off my shoulders. I came to know God at a youth club, and I was supported by the youth leaders. My addictions took a while to shake off, but as I came closer to God my desire for them began to fade. God redeemed my trust in people and gave me peace. This peace made drinking seem stupid, now that I didn't have to impress anyone! This peace took hold of my anxiety and eased it, making smoking less appealing! The more I came to know God the more I realised I was cherished and loved beyond compare, that I could be a new creation and start afresh!

It has been hard, and I've had to lose some so-called 'friends' along the way who didn't want me to change. Redemption has brought me from that broken 13-year-old to a woman of God! I now have a role in my church that I could never have dreamed of, a career, a husband, a mortgage, a purpose and peace about God's plan for my life!

Amy

CHAPTER ONE

CATCHING THE
HEART OF GOD

The journey of IAMREDEMPTION began for me during the summer of 2013. While enjoying a holiday with my family in rural France, I suddenly fell ill and was rushed into the hospital and diagnosed with appendicitis. Thankfully, they caught it in time and, after a successful operation, I woke up in a French hospital a very grateful man. Apparently the infection was very serious and had been in my body for a while. The next morning the doctor came into my room and jokingly asked, 'Are you Superman?'

'Not that I know of,' I responded. He then described that when they opened me up, they saw something they had never seen before.

'It was as if your own body was protecting you and resisting the infection that was trying to spread,' he explained. As I lay there and considered his words, I was reminded of the scriptures in the third chapter of Corinthians that say we are not mere men but temples of the Holy Ghost. I was also thankful for the way God had directed me to the right place at the right time to get this health issue sorted.

———————————

Little did I know what would also happen during my stay in that hospital. I was totally unaware that God was going to use this opportunity of me being confined to a bed to do something that would both reshape and redefine me in a very radical way. Anyone who knows me will tell you it's not an easy thing to keep me in one place for long; I like to keep busy and have a fairly short attention span. For me to be laid up for over a week was a whole new experience. The hospital was not the nicest of places for my family to be while on holiday, so I kept their daily visits short and sent them off to enjoy the rest of their day.

Day after day, as I lay resting and letting my body repair, I found myself suddenly with lots of time to think, ponder, read my Bible and pray. I hadn't considered myself in spiritual need when I went into hospital; actually, things between God and I had been pretty good. I hadn't been crying out for personal revival or a visitation from God in the days prior to our getaway. In fact, I had been simply enjoying the time unwinding as I holidayed with my family, enjoying taking time each day walking along canals, drawing close to God again after a very busy few months of ministry.

With the success of the operation over with, I was enjoying my time listening to praise and worship, reading my Bible and a good book I had brought with me. I was not expecting what would happen next. It was Saturday night about 7 pm. As I was worshipping and praying, I felt the tangible presence of God fill my hospital room. I have experienced the feeling of the presence of God at other times – especially in worship – but this was very different. As I felt the intense warmth of His presence, an incredible peace flooded me from the top of my head to the soles of my feet. I didn't understand why this was happening at first. My initial thoughts were that He was healing my body, but regardless of whether that was it or not,

I knew that I loved every moment of what was happening.

Though truly difficult to explain or put into words, try to imagine it as being in the presence of a loving father with an incredible heart full of intense love who had suddenly entered the room. All I wanted to do was soak it in. Being in ministry for over twenty years, I knew that God was doing something special in me and I didn't want it to stop. This passionate embrace of my loving Father remained with me all night, and I eventually drifted off to sleep. When I awoke early the next morning I felt very refreshed and well rested, also I was so very conscious that His presence was still there and still very strong as it was the night before. The only difference was that I was immediately conscious that something had changed in me – I felt different, I felt new! I can remember I just lay there and started to thank Him over and over again for what He had done even though I didn't fully know what that was.

I felt as though I had been operated on a second time, but this time not by men, but by God. Something had been taken out of me, something had changed deep within. I am not talking about deliverance or anything evil, just something that needed to be sorted. It was like God had taken 'infected flesh' out of me – dead stuff that had accumulated over the years or things of the world that had unknowingly polluted me. It took me a few weeks to be able to accurately put into words what had happened. All I knew was that I felt different, new, more alive than I had ever felt before.

I remember my prayer that morning, 'God, whatever you have done I don't want to lose it; whatever you have removed, I don't want it back! How do I maintain this new-ness?'

I sensed his reply, 'How are you going to maintain the removal of your appendix?'

'I'm not, I can't – it's gone.'

Then I felt Him say, 'It's the same with this. I have made all things new, now live out of what I have done in you.'

It was amazing, like I was born again – *again*. I was so in love with God, so forgiven, so clean. I suddenly understood the concept of the 'new creation' better than I ever had before and I had been preaching it for over twenty years! I had a fresh, vibrant revelation of the power of the new birth – the death of the old man – resurrection of the new man, alive in his spirit to God.

Please let me clarify that, prior to this event, I was not aware of any moral failure or gross sin in my life. Though obviously not perfect, I had always lived out what I preached the best I could. But now, I felt renewed to the extent that the guy I was the week before seemed to be so very far from God in comparison to the man that now lay in that bed. How had I drifted off course? Possibly over time, in our walk with God, things like apathy and familiarity begin to numb and disempower us. Now that I saw the difference, I never wanted to go back!

But one key thing that stood out and was the central theme of my night in God's presence was the word 'redemption'. In the midst of all that God was doing in me, He placed in my spirit a fresh understanding of His redemptive heart and love for mankind. I had read many books on redemption, would even consider myself a redemption preacher, but all of a sudden it was more than theory or theology – it was a living heartbeat. It was like I had caught the very heartbeat of God! During the time that God was operating on me, He placed in me His heartbeat of redemption for man. Not just relating to the eternal ramifications of heaven and hell, but also how He loves us and has plans of redemption, restoration and renewal for our everyday lives while we walk here on the earth.

God began to speak to me by His Spirit and through His Word that His will still is 'that none would perish'. Those old familiar words began to roar again through the corridors of my heart. He started to talk to me bluntly about things, I am embarrassed to say, I had almost forgotten. Things that were in the Bible, but I had unknowingly avoided or not taught like I maybe should have. It was like I had let them fall out of the back of the book. This would have been easy to do because they were found in the book of Revelation, the final book of the Bible.

I am speaking specifically about three things: the Lamb's book of life, the big white throne and the lake of fire that awaits those who reject Jesus. I started to get concerned – I mean, why was God speaking to me about what happens in the afterlife? Why was He impressing on me afresh the reality of these three things? It was only the warmth of His presence that assured me my time was not up! But my heart was now very stirred, and my attention fully His.

Why was He reminding me of these things I had forgotten or not taught people about as I should? Later, I realised it was because He was putting His heart afresh in me and He wanted me to know how He actually feels about people being cast into fire at the end of days. He was purging me of the Pentecostal images that had built up over the years, images that were impressed in me as a young child by 'fire and brimstone' preachers. You see, when I thought of the white throne and God casting people into the lake of fire, I pictured a man tossing wood into a wood burner. Unwittingly, I had drastically missed the revelation of the heartache God will have on that day for every single one that is lost or cast away from Him.

Now that I had the heartbeat of God, I realised that this God that created man did not want *anyone* to perish or be cast into a lake of fire; rather, He willed *all* to come to Him through His Son; for *all* to experience the redemption that He provided in Jesus. But in giving man free will, He could not force redemptive salvation upon man. Man had to choose to accept or reject the Saviour and it would be their rejection of His provided Saviour that would cause their name to remain blotted out of the Lamb's book. Instead of seeing the gates of heaven open to them, they would spend an eternity in a dreadful place of separation from Him, known to us as hell. Yet the truth remains: He made a way for all to escape this sentence of torment originated by the disobedience of Adam. Man has a choice. He lays before them the option of life and death but cannot make the choice for any man, yet desperately desires for all men to choose life! (See Deuteronomy 30:19-20.)

Now I understood, like never before, this awesome God actually longs with a deep longing for all mankind to be redeemed back into relationship with Himself – for all men to have lives that are bound for heaven to be with Him, rather than a place of torment without Him. Maybe as you are reading this you are saying, 'Wait a minute, this is a bit full on, Andy.' My friend, you need to realise, it really is. The eternal consequence for the person who rejects Christ is indeed horrific, and we must grasp the reality of this. Then we may take the Great Commission as seriously as we should, especially concerning our friends and family. It is not God's will that any would perish, not one. We carry in the message of redemption a divine invitation that holds the power to reroute a person eternally. How can we stay silent – unless we are guilty of not taking this invitation, stained with the blood of His only Son, seriously?

So, to go back to my story, there I was lying in a hospital bed in rural France. I had encountered the presence of God in a profound way and He had placed His redemptive heart into the centre of my heart. I saw afresh the realities of what lay beyond the grave for all men but was at the very same time totally overwhelmed by His massive heart of love, a heart that desires all to be saved and not destroyed. I was pondering things I had long ago forgotten – the big white throne, the Lamb's book of life and the lake of fire. At this point I began to think, how do I tell Gina about this? She'll think I've gone bonkers or that they have overdosed me on painkillers! As I considered how to approach the subject with Gina, the door opened and in she walked. She had left the kids at the holiday accommodation under the care of my oldest daughter. This certainly made it easier to talk honestly to her about my experience.

She could sense straight away that something had happened and started to ask what was going on, fearing the doctors had told me something dreadful. So, I took a deep breath and began to tell her about what I had experienced – how God had done an unexpected mighty work in me, how I felt alive and more of a new creation than ever before. As she sat there looking at me, I blurted out, 'Gina, God has been talking to me about the big white throne, the Lamb's book of life and the lake of fire! God does not want anyone to know those flames; He passionately loves all man and wants none to perish.'

Then it was my turn to be surprised as she looked up at me with tears in her eyes and said, 'Last night I had a dream . . .'

Now to understand the impact of those words, you have to know that Gina rarely dreams – I dream all the time – but not Gina. We often laugh that I have a whole other world that waits for me when I close my eyes, and my dreams are incredibly real. Gina hardly ever dreams.

But the night before, she had a dream that stunned me. I am a firm believer that God sees a man and wife as one and when He is saying something profound that will affect the future of that couple, He will speak to them both to confirm His word. She began to tell me that in her dream she was in a big white room and was conscious of a very hot fire burning and, though she could not see them, she was aware of the presence of a father and a son. She heard the son saying, 'Dad, this is going to burn, isn't it? Dad, this is going to hurt – Dad, you can't help me now, can you?'

She heard the father's voice respond sadly, 'No, son, I can't help. It is going to hurt, but there is nothing that I can do now, it's too late.' She told me that the father's voice did not sound angry, but loving and very sad. She compared it to the emotions of a parent of a son who had committed a crime and had been found guilty by the court. The parent could not stop the given punishment because the law had been broken, yet also was the one that had to deliver their child to the prison. In reality, in the same way God has made a way for all to be saved and forgiven but He can't make them choose that way. I fervently believe that right up to a person's very last breath, God will do everything He can to guide us to that choice, but when our last breath is breathed it's simply too late to change decisions made.

As Gina and I sat there after these revelations, we both cried as we realised God was doing something that would redefine us and impact the churches He had entrusted us to lead, far beyond the moment we were in. That weekend, God placed in us His heart of redemption, and since then I have not been able to feel the same about people and communities, and for that I am so very thankful. I want to pass this heartbeat, a heartbeat of God's redemptive love for people, onto as many as I can. Will you catch God's heartbeat? Will you allow Him to place His redemptive heart for humanity in you? A redemptive heart that does not just concern itself with a person's eternal destiny but reaches into their present life as well? A heart that desires to mend those who are broken, restore those who are damaged, and renew hope where hope has been lost? Who loves to make all things new, and has the power to do exactly that in the life that reaches out to Him? Will you dare to be a carrier of His redemptive heart?

IAMREDEMP†ION.org STORIES

From religion to relationship

I was brought up a Catholic, but I never had a personal relationship with God, or even knew I could! Growing up my Dad was always very strict and not outwardly affectionate and, at 15 years of age, I believed that he didn't love me. I felt like I wasn't understood by my Mum either.

I became hurt and hard-hearted. I looked for attention and wanting to belong in the wrong places. I started smoking, drinking and also taking drugs. I got involved with the wrong people and soon the drugs started to take over my life, so much so that I lost myself and became a shadow of myself. I messed up my A-Levels which resulted in me getting kicked out of home. I lived in some horrible places, knowing there was more to my life. I eventually moved back home and went to College. During this time I didn't have a lot of friends and my life was rubbish.

My Nan gave me a daily devotional book, which was key in me turning to God. One day I was so unhappy with my life, I cried out to Jesus and after this I found myself repenting to God for all my past sin. I then had an encounter with God. While I was sleeping, a picture of Jesus was so bright that I could not keep my eyes shut. I remember being jolted upright in my bed – speaking in tongues – something that I had never even heard of!

I finished College and went to University in Liverpool. I went to churches but hadn't encountered God again, until a friend invited me to her church. It was here that, in worship, I encountered God as we sang about His love. It was being a part of this church that I was restored and transformed. I now know how loved I am, and I have a wonderful husband and beautiful baby girl. Also, the relationship with my parents and sisters is better than it's ever been. I have seen two of my younger sisters come to know God as well, which is awesome. Praise God!

Jenny

CHAPTER TWO

REDEMPTION
IS A BIG WORD

We've established that God is a God of redemption, but what does that actually mean? What is redemption?

Redemption is one of those massive words that have such richness of meaning; I remember seeing this word throughout my time of knowing God but never fully grasped it till now. I had seen it on hymn books growing up – *Redemption Hymnal*. I had heard the word in certain songs we sang in church and in messages the minister would speak, but only now has the full power of this word come into my understanding. It is a life-changing word worthy of getting excited about. As you can tell I *am* excited by it and I want to get you excited about it too!

WHAT IS REDEMPTION?

There are many different dictionary definitions for redemption but, simply put, redemption means to purchase or restore back to an original owner or condition, to make new and alive again.

WORLD ENGLISH DICTIONARY:

- to recover possession or ownership of by payment of a price or service; regain;
- to pay off (a debt, promissory note, loan, etc.);
- to recover;
- to reinstate in someone's estimation or good opinion, restore to favour;
- to make amends for – to recover from captivity, by a payment.

When it comes to our salvation, this is certainly a great definition and true example of the word. Our salvation is simply that: a story of redemption. We were made by God, lost from God and then purchased back to God at His own cost.

We were all separated from God by the disobedience of Adam, but have been united back to God through the obedience of Christ. Just as all humanity was lost from God in the actions of the one man Adam, so all humanity has been purchased back to God in the actions of one man, Jesus. His blood was full payment to redeem (purchase) man back to his creator.

> Therefore, just as through one man sin entered the world, and death through sin, and thus death spread to all men, because all sinned – (for until the law sin was in the world, but sin is not imputed when there is no law. Nevertheless death reigned from Adam to Moses, even over those who had not sinned according to the likeness of the transgression of Adam, who is a type of Him who was to come. But the free gift is not like the offense. For if by the one man's offense many died, much more the grace of God and the gift by the grace of the one Man, Jesus Christ, abounded to many. And the gift is not like that which came through the one who sinned. For the judgement which came from one offense resulted in condemnation, but the free gift which came from many offenses resulted in justification. For if by the one man's offense death reigned through the one, much more those who receive abundance of grace and of the gift of righteousness will reign in life

through the One, Jesus Christ.) Therefore, as through one man's offense judgement came to all men, resulting in condemnation, even so through one Man's righteous act the free gift came to all men, resulting in justification of life. For as by one man's disobedience many were made sinners, so also by one Man's obedience many will be made righteous.

Romans 5:12-19

In Him (Jesus) we have redemption through His blood, the forgiveness of sins, according to the riches of His grace.
Ephesians 1:7

Maybe you are asking, if all humanity was paid for by the single sacrificial act of Jesus, then everyone's saved right? Sadly no, it takes an act of faith to enter into the eternal redemption God has provided. Legally all men are paid for, but it only becomes vital or reality when the individual believes, and puts their faith in what Jesus did for them personally.

The moment they believe in their heart and confess with their mouths Christ as Saviour, they are instantly redeemed, made alive to God; having all their trespasses forgiven.

If you confess with your mouth the Lord Jesus and believe in your heart that God has raised Him from the dead, you will be saved. For with the heart one believes unto righteousness, and with the mouth confession is made unto salvation.

Romans 10:9-10

> And he brought them out and said, 'Sirs, what must I do
> to be saved?' So they said, 'Believe on the Lord Jesus
> Christ, and you will be saved, you and your household.'
> **Acts 16:30-31**

To paint a real simple picture of godly redemption, especially concerning restoring humanity back to Himself at His own cost, let me share with you a story I once heard.

A STORY OF REDEMPTION

There was once a man who made a hobby of building boats. Specifically, he would build boats out of used matchsticks. He had built many over the years but had just finished his most favourite ship of all. He had spent hours pouring his creative heart into this galleon. Many hours and matchsticks, and much patience had created a masterpiece which was now his most prized possession. Formed with his own hand, this vessel demonstrated his fullest creative ability.

After being housebound for many months due to building the boat, he left to get some food to celebrate, leaving the ship on the kitchen table. While away, some thieves broke into his home, ransacked his house, stole his valuables and prepared to leave. Just as they were exiting, one of the thieves spotted the boat on the table and took a liking to it. Being a heartless thief, he did not stop to consider the feelings of the man who had made it. Rather, he saw the opportunity to take it as well as the other valuables they had found.

A little later the man returned to find his house had been burgled. He looked around and noticed things that were missing – televisions and other electrical equipment. Suddenly his boat came to mind and, running into the kitchen, his heart sank as he saw the now empty place where his masterpiece once proudly sat. Though distressed with the other belongings that had been taken, this hurt him the most. Why? It's because he had poured himself into this creation. Upset, he reported it to the police; statements were made, but not much hope given.

A few weeks later, the man was walking through his local high street. As he passed a pawn shop, his eye was attracted to something familiar. Stopping to look again, he noticed his beloved ship in the window. Obviously, the thief had valued its monetary worth more than its artistry and had pawned the boat along with some other things that had been stolen. Excitedly, the man ran in and called for the shopkeeper. He explained how the boat was previously his and how it had been taken. To his surprise, the shopkeeper, though happy for him, explained how it was now his property and a payment would be needed to regain ownership of the ship he loved. When the man asked the price to redeem or buy back what actually belonged to him, the shopkeeper, being an opportunist, raised the price far higher than the boat was considered to be worth. Seeing the desire in the customer's eyes to re-own what he had created, he purposefully set a price that was very high. Then, it was the shopkeeper who was surprised as the man nodded and left the shop, telling

him he would be back after visiting the bank. Within the hour the man returned and, without any bartering, paid the man the full price he had quoted. The shopkeeper, with a confused expression, bewildered that the man had not tried to bargain, handed the man his ship. As he placed the overpayment of cash into the register, he watched as the man left the shop. On leaving he heard him say to the boat that was again in his possession, 'I made you, and I bought you back. You are twice mine.'

This simplest of stories holds the very essence of the gospel. The good news that we believe, because what we read in the Bible, is the good news of redemption. A true story of the redemptive heart of God concerning us, and the lengths He would go to get us back to Himself. After we were stolen through deception, He paid the greatest price of all, the blood of His only beloved son Jesus.

> Knowing that you were not redeemed with corruptible things, like silver or gold, from your aimless conduct received by tradition from your fathers, but with the precious blood of Christ, as of a lamb without blemish and without spot.
>
> **1 Peter 1:18-19**

A BIGGER WORD

So to be redeemed means to be purchased back, to have debt settled; to be restored to your original owner, the lover of your soul. But when you begin to chew on and savour the word redemption, you suddenly find more flavour than you first noticed.

You see, redemption is the very heartbeat of God; it is not just what He does but who He is. It fully describes His intentions for us, intentions that are indeed redemptive; among other things, it means to make new, fresh, alive again, to restore what is broken, revive what is dead, to make brand new. Whenever you see God do something redemptive in the Bible, you always see new beginnings and restored people. A great example of this is our salvation. In redeeming us, God never had a plan to patch us up and leave us confined to a life of never-ending behaviour management. No, He always had a new creation in mind, a fresh new birth experience for those who would believe in Him.

Listen to how Paul explains it in 2 Corinthians:

> Therefore, if anyone is in Christ, he is a new creation; old things have passed away; behold, all things have become new. Now all things are of God, who has reconciled us to Himself through Jesus Christ, and has given us the ministry of reconciliation.
>
> **2 Corinthians 5:17-18**

Many Christians do not live in the fullness of their redemption because they are still, often unconsciously, trying to maintain the life of a former existence instead of living out from the platform of being a new creation. Jesus never died to patch up an old you, but rather provided a doorway of new birth, so that you could leave the old you buried behind, and step into a new resurrected you, which was forgiven and raised to newness of life in Christ.

Look how Paul again clearly separates the two existences of a person's life:

What shall we say then? Are we to continue in sin so that grace may increase? May it never be! How shall we who died to sin still live in it? Or do you not know that all of us who have been baptised into Christ Jesus have been baptised into His death? Therefore we have been buried with Him through baptism into death, so that as Christ was raised from the dead through the glory of the Father, so we too might walk in newness of life. For if we have become united with Him in the likeness of His death, certainly we shall also be in the likeness of His resurrection, knowing this, that our old self was crucified with Him, in order that our body of sin might be done away with, so that we would no longer be slaves to sin; for he who has died is freed from sin. Now if we have died with Christ, we believe that we shall also live with Him, knowing that Christ, having been raised from the dead, is never to die again; death no longer is master over Him. For the death that He died, He died to sin once for all; but the life that He lives, He lives to God. Even so consider yourselves to be dead to sin, but alive to God in Christ Jesus.

Romans 6:1-11 (NASB)

Through the new birth we died to what we were, being totally separated from the power of sin that once controlled and ruled us. We were buried, meaning the old man was done away with. This verse runs in complete agreement with what we read in 2 Corinthians when it says, *'old things have passed away'*. Think about it, that expression is one that we only use at funerals when we say, 'Brother Albert has passed away.' What do we mean by that? Simply that brother Albert is gone; you will never see him or experience him ever again in this life. That, my friend, is the power of God's redemptive plan for us. He kills and buries who we used to be, rather than strapping them to our backs to be managed by us. Then comes the third component of this incredible truth, the most important: we are then raised to newness of life in Him. The power of living successfully in your God-given new creation life is found in verse 11: *'Even so consider yourself dead to who you were and alive to who God has made you to be through new birth.'*

The reality is that your old man – the old you – was crucified with Christ. That means he is dead, no longer in existence beyond what you allow him to be – through things like ignorance and stubbornness. God never had a patch-up plan for your life, but a new beginning. Jesus was a doorway to a fresh start, a start that finds its first day in the freedom from sin He provides through death. Our new birth was always the redemptive master plan of God through Christ.

> Jesus answered and said to him, 'Most assuredly, I say to you, unless one is born again, he cannot see the kingdom of God.' Nicodemus said to Him, 'How can a man be born when he is old? Can he enter a second time into his mother's womb and be born?' Jesus answered, 'Most assuredly, I say to you, unless one is born of water and the Spirit, he cannot enter the kingdom of God. That which is born of the flesh is flesh, and that which is born of the Spirit is spirit.'
>
> **John 3:3-6**

REDEMPTION MAKES NEW; RESTORES, MAKES ALIVE AGAIN THAT WHICH WAS DEAD

> And you He made alive, who were dead in trespasses and sin.
>
> **Ephesians 2:1**

> Even when we were dead in trespasses, made us alive together with Christ (by grace you have been saved).
>
> **Ephesians 2:5**

> And you, being dead in your trespasses and the

uncircumcision of your flesh, He has made alive together
with Him, having forgiven you all trespasses.
Colossians 2:13

REDEMPTION AFFECTS OUR LIFE HERE, NOT JUST THE ONE TO COME

When it comes to understanding God's redemptive heart, it is vital for us to grasp that His redemptive plans for us don't just relate to what happens when we die or end at the miracle of our new birth, but also affect everything in the lives we live here. God cares about us and has redemptive intentions for sickness to be turned to health, lack to be replaced with abundance and broken relationships to be restored. God cares about the lives we live now. And as it says in Jeremiah 29:11, He has plans to prosper, give a future and a hope. What I am saying is simply this: God loves you and has redemptive intentions of restoration for those areas in your life that presently seem broken, destroyed or in ruins.

REDEMPTION IS THE THEME OF THE BIBLE

The word redemption not only reveals to us the very heart of God but it is also the overriding theme of the entire Bible, from Genesis to Revelation. There is one constant theme – you guessed it – redemption! The truth is that you will never know God as you should if you don't understand the redemptive heart He has for man. Equally, you will never understand the Bible as you could unless you read it in the light of redemption.

By this I mean that as you read it, understanding the constant theme that runs through it, you will then suddenly see that all the little stories and accounts that seemed so random and unconnected will join together and declare one common shout of truth: 'God is a redemptive God'.

After considering this, watch how many of the stories will now make sense that did not before! These stories were purposefully included by God to enable Him to reveal the many facets of His ever redemptive heart of love for man. Allow me to grab a couple of examples to show you what I mean.

HOSEA

The prophet Hosea was called to marry an unfaithful wife. This to me was always a very strange book in the Bible, and one could wonder why it's there. Basically, God tells one of His prophets to marry a 'loose woman', who was similar to a prostitute in her unfaithfulness to her husband. Through this marriage God wanted to show Israel the love He had for her even though she was like an unfaithful wife towards Him. (Poor Hosea! I'm so glad I didn't get this mission!) He marries her as per God's instruction and, though he faithfully loves her, she cheats on him time and time again. He keeps taking her back and washing her with his restoring love – and she keeps breaking his trust! What a painful cycle this must have been for the heart of this man. Eventually, as it has been portrayed in some good films, we see her standing in the marketplace once again but, this time, no one is bidding. Her youth has gone and her looks have faded; she is not visibly desirable like once she was. Naked, she stands on an auction block with no man wanting to bid – she is used, unwanted. Then suddenly, the crowd parts and a man steps forward, he bids full price for her without bartering. It is Hosea, her faithful husband. He looks at her and says, 'I will have you; I have never stopped loving you or wanting you. Come home with me, my love, you are adored.'

In this account we see the redemptive heart of God displayed towards an unfaithful Israel – but it's also for us. How many times have we not been true to Him who loves us, or allowed our lives to become what they were never meant to be? When others have walked away or abandoned us, we hear in the marketplace of our failure and stupidity, the voice of a redemptive God that says, 'Come home with me my love, I have plans for you . . . plans to restore, make new and provide fresh beginnings.'

RUTH AND BOAZ

In this next account we read about Boaz, a man fittingly called the 'kinsman redeemer'. The story of Ruth is one of loss and faithfulness. She is happily married to a man, has a great life, then suddenly her husband and his brother die, and she and her sister-in-law become widows. Her mother-in-law, Naomi, tells the women that they are free to go now that her sons are dead, because she had no future to offer them. One woman takes her up on her offer and leaves, but

Ruth loyally refuses and pledges to stay and care for the mother of her late husband. She displays faithfulness that I believe caught the attention of God. As we read on we see them struggle, Ruth nearly begging to bring in enough to support them. Her once safe life of being loved and cared for by a strong man was now apparently gone forever. To survive, she was forced to glean the heads of grain from the outside edge of local fields. These gleanings were normally left for the poor to collect and, as long as they didn't touch the crop, they were allowed the leftovers.

One day, Boaz noticed the lovely Ruth gathering at the edge of the field and inquired of her. He discovered that because of her husband's death she legally belonged to another. He met with the man and made a redemptive deal to win her to himself; basically, he buys the field to gain this girl. He makes her his own and redeems her life. She is once again restored from one of a broken person with no one to care for her, to a lady protected, cherished and safe again. Take time to read this Bible story as it is a beautiful declaration of the heart of God towards us. He loves us so much He will 'buy the field' to gain the heart of who we are. He will take on a life, often messy and broken, to gain the person because He has love-inspired redemptive intentions for their life.

MEPHIBOSHETH, THE SON OF JONATHAN

In 2 Samuel we read of a young man who was the son of Jonathan, and the grandson of Saul. In chapter four we notice that, at the age of five, he was dropped by a nurse and became crippled in his legs. Reading further, we note that he was warned that King David would only do him harm if found, as he was the only living relative of the former king. Consequently, he spent his life in fear and hiding from David. What he didn't know was that David actually had redemptive intentions concerning him. As we see in chapter nine, David inquired whether there was any offspring of Saul and Jonathan that he may show covenant kindness to. He is then informed of the disabled son of his best friend Jonathan, who died in battle. He immediately released horsemen to find this boy so that he could bless his life and do him good. The sad bit is that as they look for him they can't find him because he is hiding; hiding because of what others had told him concerning King David. He had been told that David was bad, and would only do him harm. This was so far from the truth it was ridiculous. David had been severely misrepresented to him. Eventually David's horsemen found Mephibosheth and told him of David's good intentions; they scooped him up and took him to David's palace. When he entered, he bowed down in fear because of what others had told him about David. But we see David lift him up, bless him and bring restoration to his life.

> Now when Mephibosheth the son of Jonathan, the son of Saul, had come to David, he fell on his face and prostrated himself. Then David said, 'Mephibosheth?'

> And he answered, 'Here is your servant!' So David said
> to him, 'Do not fear, for I will surely show you kindness
> for Jonathan your father's sake, and will restore to you
> all the land of Saul your grandfather; and you shall eat
> bread at my table continually.'
>
> 'As for Mephibosheth,' said the king, 'he shall eat at my
> table like one of the king's sons.'
> **2 Samuel 9:6-7, 11**

David had made a covenant with his father, Jonathan, and a covenant meant that he would care for the offspring of Jonathan. On remembering this covenant, he looked for the disabled son with redemptive intention, not with thoughts of harm, but thoughts of kindness and restoration.

Here again we can see many redemptive comparisons:

Like Mephibosheth, so many people today are crippled by the actions of another. The injuries to his legs were the result of the negligence of another. How often do you meet people that are limping (emotionally, relationally or even spiritually) because of what someone else did to them? Like David's heart towards Mephibosheth, God has a plan of restoration towards them to mend them and do them good.

Because of how others had misrepresented David, this young man hid from his messengers sent to bless him. So, too, people are hiding from God today instead of running to Him because of how He has been misrepresented. We need to make sure that we are the horsemen of God in our society, messengers that carry good news of restoration and not threats of judgement and torment.

As Mephibosheth was restored to the king's table, so will every person that responds to the invitation of the King of Kings. Consider the fact that when this crippled boy sat at the table of David, his broken legs were covered by the table cloth and he looked just like anyone else. God's table is so much better than David's. He doesn't just cover the broken legs of men, but rather restores and heals them so they can walk again! When you sit with God at His table, your wounds are healed and your breaks are mended. He redeems what was destroyed regardless of how it happened.

These are just three stories, but as you continue to read the Word of God, you will see story after story revealing to the reader over and over again the redemptive heart of a loving Father; a God whose will is that none would perish in their earthly lives as well as their eternal one. We need to carry not just the message of our redemptive God, but His heart as well, so that we would see people and the situations they are facing through His eyes. I believe that Jesus sums up the redemptive heart of His father well in the book of Revelation:

> Then He who sat on the throne said, 'Behold, I make all things new.' And He said to me, 'Write, for these words are true and faithful.'
>
> **Revelation 21:5**

Redemption does exactly that – it makes all things new. We have just mentioned accounts taken from the Old Testament, but we see the manifestation of the redemptive intentions of God towards man all the way through the old and the new – and none more than through the ministry of Jesus Christ. Everywhere Christ the redeemer went, lives were changed. Whether it was the woman caught in adultery, saved and given a new beginning, or the multiple lepers healed and their life restored; time and time again in every page of the gospels, we see lives healed, restored and made free. Why? It is because Jesus was the personification of the redemptive heart of His father. He was God's heart made flesh; a heart that beat for the well-being and restoration of the humanity He never stopped loving.

THE GREAT I AM

When He walked the earth in His bodily form, Jesus revealed Himself in many ways. Among other things, He said of Himself that He was the doorway back to God (John 10:9); the bread of life (John 6:35, 48); the good shepherd (John 10:11). But one of my favourites is when He called Himself the great I AM. He was speaking to a nation that saw Abraham as their spiritual father. Jesus shocks them by placing His own existence before that of Abraham.

> Jesus said to them, 'Most assuredly, I say to you, before Abraham was, I AM.'
>
> **John 8:58**

Jesus was and is and always will be the great I AM. He is 'I AM healer' to the sick, 'I AM Saviour' to the lost, and 'I AM redemption' to all humanity. You see, Christ the Redeemer is not just a statue in Rio De Janeiro, Brazil. Rather, Christ the Redeemer is a living God who was, and is, and is to come. And, like the image of the statue, the living Christ extends His arms to a broken world declaring to it: 'IAMREDEMPTION!'

IAMREDEMP†ION.org STORIES

Walking away from gang culture

I've always known that God existed and Jesus Christ was Lord and Saviour, as I had grown up in a church, and my father is a pastor. However, this didn't always mean that I was living a life that acknowledged and declared His glory. I always felt God speaking to me and saving me from situations. All this was happening as I was living a half-empty life and more concerned about the material things to gain in the world.

I grew up in South-east London, and by my early teens I fell into the gang life culture of selling drugs, carrying weapons, getting arrested and meaningless sex. All this life brought for me was two stabbings and a near shooting. However, in the midst of all this mess, God was still standing by me and saving me. There were times where I would just miss someone who would want to harm me by minutes and in these times I felt God saying, "I still love you, my child".

This life went on until I got arrested when I was 17 and had my motorbike taken away from me. In that time I sat alone in the cell, though it wasn't my first time, I felt God saying to me, "There is a way out...." Not long after I was released I decided that I couldn't live this life anymore, as the spirit of conviction had fallen upon me. I started to pray more and seek God more, and more opportunities began to arise, most particularly through refereeing football, which ultimately helped me drop my past.

Though I had stopped living my previous life, I was still living half-empty for Christ, until New Years Eve 2012 when, in a service during worship, I felt God softly saying, "Give it all to me, it's in my hands". At that point I knew it was time I devoted my life to Christ without turning back to old ways. By March 2013 I was baptised and, as time went on and I sought after God more and more, I felt – and continue to feel – Him guiding me with every step I take. I couldn't have asked for anything better.

Josh

CHAPTER THREE

'LET THE REDEEMED OF THE LORD SAY SO'

> Let the redeemed of the LORD say so, whom He has
> redeemed from the hand of the enemy.
>
> **Psalm 107:2**

I believe this is a very relevant passage of scripture for the church today, a church that sadly seems to have become too silent when it comes to telling others about what God has done for them. It is a church that desperately needs to be mobilised again; to be carriers of the redemptive heart of God to their generation. I have known of this verse in the Bible since childhood but as I have journeyed forward in my understanding of redemption it has become freshly profound. I recently read this verse in a different translation of the Bible, causing it come to life again and light up in a whole new way:

> Let the redeemed of the LORD tell their story.
>
> **Psalm 107:2 (NIV)**

IT'S TIME TO TELL YOUR STORY

If you are a Christian, then you have been redeemed. As we established previously, redemption has produced your salvation and given you a solid assurance concerning where you will spend eternity. But there's so much more. Truth be told, if you sat down and thought for a while, you would begin to remember all the other moments of godly redemption in your life. Maybe there were moments when God healed you, or restored a relationship in your life. There may be times when He made a way where there seemed to be no way, or caused something that seemed dead to live again. Possibly there were opportunities that seemed ruined and then were turned around for your good. Let's be honest – we all have stories that display the goodness, kindness and redemptive heart of God towards us, don't we? The problem is that we often keep these stories a secret; we deposit them in our memory bank of inner thankfulness instead of doing something better and much more productive with them, telling others!

When I look back over the storyline of my life, I can see so clearly the moment when God stepped in and caused my life to be re-routed to a better destination and future. My story, as so many other people, was very similar to that of the redemptive story of the wayward child found in Luke 15. My family had found faith when I was about nine years old and I attended church and loved God in a childlike way till I was sixteen. At that age, the most stupid mistake I made was to believe the advertising of my friends that the world had more to offer me. So I left church to pursue the life my friends were seemingly enjoying. For the next eight years I was away from God. I could fill a book with those years and it would be a very interesting read, believe me! Suffice to say, I lived a crazy life, but I didn't realise the slow rot that was taking place in me. At the age of twenty-four I fell on my knees a broken young man – confused, addicted, embarrassed of the person I had become, and so much more. I called out to the God I had known as a boy and purposed, like the wayward son in the Gospel of Luke, to return my life to God the Father. Just like the story, when I returned home I found a Father that loved me and welcomed me back with open arms. Over the years that followed, He restored my life in every way possible; that was over twenty-five years ago.

When I look back over the time-line of my life I see the powerful redemptive intentions of God at work. When looking at your life, don't you agree? As a young man, my life was heading nowhere. In hindsight, I believe I had pressed a self-destruct button much earlier on as I veered stupidly away from God. My life was heading for a sure and certain fall off the cliff of total destruction. Someone asked me once where would I be today without God. I answered almost immediately: one of three places – dead, in prison or sick in hospital – because the reckless pace I was living at was not sustainable. I can see that so clearly now but, at the time, I was blinded with deception and my future actually meant nothing to me.

I was such a mess, I was a thief, I didn't know how to love, whether it be a relationship or a dream; I broke everything I touched. I had the opposite to the Midas touch – everything I touched turned to dung! I had no purpose in life, content to sell fruit and vegetables by day and sing in the pubs at night. That was the extent of my vision for the rest of my life. Then, at the age of twenty-four, I encountered Christ the redeemer. He stepped back into the driver's seat of my life and began to slowly but surely steer it in a better direction. Very soon my life was coming into new freedom as addictions were super-naturally being broken, life-controlling patterns radically changed. And all of this was happening from the inside out! This is what made it sustainable rather than momentary. You see, I wasn't making it happen externally – it was flowing from a new life within. The story of my life changed the day I gave my life back to God and has kept on changing ever since. How about you? Take a moment to think about how God stepped into your storyline and how He has re-routed your life too.

Today, I am not addicted to anything but God! I've been very happily married now for over twenty years, with five beautiful kids that love the Lord. Am I boasting? Yes! But I'm not boasting in me, but in Him. I remember painfully well what I was when He found me. I know that the old Andy could not be a faithful husband or stay in a relationship longer than a few months; he would have been a very self-centred man, who wouldn't have cared or taken the time to raise kids in a godly way. When I look in the mirror today, I see a transformed life – a reborn person – a 'God-changed' story!

When a person receives Christ the redeemer, the storyline changes. Though it can sometimes be confusing as it is being re-written, later, when you flick back over the story of your life, you will see how the incredible hand of God changed things for the better. Every one of us has a great story. We aren't meant to keep it 'a best kept secret' though! We're supposed to tell others about what God has done. As we do, we turn their hearts and their hopelessness to Him. We lead them by our testimony to the divine story-changer, so that they can have a story-change in their life, too. But if we stay silent, if we don't tell our story, how will they know? It's time for the redeemed of the Lord to tell their story! Will you begin to tell yours?

One of the many things that separate us from false cults and mere religions is that we have a personal testimony of what God has done and is still doing for us. If you ask a Jehovah's Witness, for example, what God has done for them recently, you will usually get a blank expression because they have no personal experiences, just false teachings based on deceptive theories that have been drilled into them to repeat in a desperate endeavour to obtain a chance of salvation. The followers have no personal stories of redemption in their own lives! But we – we have stories! Stories of what God did when He saved us; stories of circumstances turned around; stories of how God made a way for us when there seemed to be no way. These stories really need to be told!

IAMREDEMPTION IS ALL ABOUT TELLING OUR STORIES

When God placed this fresh understanding of His redemptive heart for man in me, one of the first things I wanted to do was tell someone. That's a natural reaction to something good happening in your life, right? The next thing I wanted to do was mobilise the people of God so they could begin to tell their unique stories too, because these stories, told by everyday people, turn the hearts of those who don't know God towards Him.

When I launched the initiative of IAMREDEMPTION, it had a dual purpose. Its impact, like a two-edged sword, was to firstly *inspire* God's people to tell their own story of redemption. To encourage them to stand up in their world and say 'IAMREDEMPTION' in that they are a recipient, they have received redemption from God.

As a ministry, one of the tools we use to do this is a website. As a person opens the IAMREDEMPTION.org website, they are welcomed by story upon story of everyday people's lives that have been changed, with each one declaring that God is real and is still a redeeming God. So many people have visited this site and have been inspired by the real life stories they found on it. It also exists to provide teaching and inspiration on how to tell your story to others.

The second edge or purpose of the site was to challenge people to *be* redemption in the lives of others. It challenges them to let God use them to be the practical hands and feet of redemption in the lives of other people and communities. We will discuss more about that in the next chapter. Why not take a minute to look at the website, especially if you've believed or been told that God doesn't work in people's lives today.

The whole thrust of IAMREDEMPTION is simply one that runs parallel with what we have always known as the Great Commission – this being a mandate given by Jesus for the church to go and tell the world about His redemptive Father.

The trouble is that much of the modern-day attractional church has sadly wandered from mobilising the church to go and be storytellers in their world. They seem more obsessed with helping people to be comfortably seated and entertained. The church was never meant to be a 'people storage unit' but rather a place that reached people, equipped people and sent people to be witnesses for God in their everyday world.

DEMYSTIFYING THE GREAT COMMISSION

Often when you hear the Great Commission preached, it can seem too scary, unattainable; something that is for church leaders only. The opposite is the truth, as the Great Commission was given to every person that belongs to God, not just their leaders! It is a desire-based mandate that simply commissions those who have experienced redemption, to go and tell their story to others. And, as they do, the power of the Holy Ghost accompanies them, providing them everything they need to do it effectively. Let's look at the Great Commission again.

> And He said to them, 'Go into all the world and preach the gospel to every creature.'
> **Mark 16:15**

> 'But you shall receive power when the Holy Spirit has come upon you; and you shall be witnesses to Me in Jerusalem, and in all Judea and Samaria, and to the end of the earth.'
> **Acts 1:8**

In these two classic commission verses we see two simple things:

We are commissioned by God to *go*, not stay. And in our going, we are simply to be witnesses of the good news of what God has provided in Jesus, as evidenced by what He has done in our lives.

God wants us to be *ready* to tell our story, not just when we go on a mission trip to the ends of the earth, but **daily in the everyday world around us**. Being a missionary is not something we do for two weeks every now and then; rather, it is the very lifestyle of the believer. We want God to use us as the vehicles that carry His redemptive heart into the lives of others – and He will.

I have always been an evangelist by calling and there is indeed a responsibility for an evangelist to win people to Christ. But when you read Ephesians 4, you see that the evangelist, as well as being a personal soul winner, is also anointed and appointed by God to equip the saints or train others in being great soul winners. I love to do this any time I get the opportunity and find it a very natural thing to do.

Often when I start to train people in evangelism, I see the fear in people's eyes concerning it. They always ask questions like how to get started; where do they begin with this gigantic commission given by Jesus. They ask, *how do I, an everyday person, go into all the world?*

My answer is always simply this: start with *your* world. Notice in the verse from the book of Acts above, that Jerusalem comes first on the list of places to go. Jerusalem does not literally mean the place in Israel, but it represents the everyday world you live in. Every person has a world unique to them. I'm not negating short-term mission trips but, rather, see your everyday life as the world that Jesus has called you to have an impact on as well. You see, your world really is unique to you – your friends, family, work associates, the people in your neighbourhood. What a circle of influence you already have! Your world may overlap with other people's worlds in certain places through common friendships, but it still very much remains your unique world.

Imagine if every person concentrated on reaching their individual world for Jesus and stopped worrying about where they think they should be going. The impact we could have would be amazing. If people thought more along the lines of you reach your world and I will reach my world, maybe the whole world would be reached a lot faster? Feel yourself relaxing, as all I am doing is making the Great Commission much less scary.

The next question normally is *how does someone like me get started with preaching the gospel?* Again, let's start by putting that into an easier, more user-friendly language. What if the scripture said, 'Go and tell your story'? Because the truth is, your story tells of Christ the redeemer and the powerful redemptive work He has done in you. Your personal story should display the gospel message in its fullness. There is nothing more authentic than a person's testimony, because they have the greatest confidence in it. Why? Because they were there when it happened. They were witnesses to what took place. That's why Jesus said in Acts that we are to be witnesses. Witnesses to what we have seen and experienced for ourselves.

IAMREDEMPTION is a mandate; it is a call for you to stand up in your life. Not to preach dead sermons or ramble off facts that don't mean much to anyone with a real need, but to stand up and begin to tell others what Jesus has done for you. Believe me, your story will turn heads and catch the attention of those in the world that God has carefully positioned you alongside.

CREATING OPPORTUNITIES

The Bible says in Proverbs 11:30, 'He who wins souls is wise.' This is a great little nugget of truth concerning being an effective soul winner. I personally don't believe that God wants everyone to get themselves a wooden box and go preach aggressively to passing crowds in the local shopping precinct. Rather, I believe He wants you to believe and be always ready for the opportunities He will provide and with wisdom also dare to create opportunities in your everyday world for sharing your story of redemption with others.

Winning people to Christ is very much like fishing. That is why I believe among those He called, Jesus called fishermen. Remember what He said to a couple of fishermen He found in Matthew 4:19, 'Come with me and I will teach you how to fish for men.' I personally think Jesus would sit and watch these fishermen and loved their patience, skill and wisdom. These things made them great candidates for his human fishing team. Think about the wisdom of a fisherman, among other things:

- they know how to use different bait to catch different fish;
- they use different nets, lines and hooks and will fish in certain places at certain times.

All God wants us to do is be just as wise as we fish for men: a friendly meal, a worship CD playing in the car, a Bible or other good quality literature strategically placed on your desk, are all ways of getting into initial conversations. Let's face it – the hard part about sharing your faith is often just getting the conversation going, right? You need to remember when God has set up an opportunity, once started, it soon takes on a life of its own and you begin to hear yourself saying things that you don't remember ever learning – that's God's Spirit working in and through you.

One of the main reasons we created the IAMREDEMPTION merchandise was simply for this purpose – to create opportunities and starting-block moments. Many people I knew said they didn't know how to initiate the opportunity to tell their story. So whether it was an IAMREDEMPTION wristband or T-shirt, we found it soon helped to initiate those conversations for them. For example:

imagine you are with a friend and they look at your wristband and, reading it, ask what it is about. You can then respond with something like, 'You know everyone has a story to their life that can be interesting, let me tell you about mine . . .' and you are off to a great start! Before long, you've become very comfortable telling people the story of how Christ the Redeemer turned your life around. Honestly, it usually is only the initial starting point that people actually find awkward, but after daring to share your story a few times, that fear soon disappears and a confidence rises and you become unstoppable!

No one is trying to send you out knocking on strangers' doors like some fanatic that normally always arrives just at the precise moment when everyone is having their dinner and trying to relax. There are wiser and more effective ways to get into conversations with people in your world. And remember, the first people you should want to share your redemption story with are those who are in your daily walk of life and already know you. These people often need only the simplest of promptings, and will allow you great grace in letting you share, especially when they see you are so passionate about it.

So why not believe God for opportunities, and start being creative in making opportunities, letting it naturally simply flow from a heart that wants others to know the story of their lives changed too. Not driven by a negative sense of obligation, but rather a desire to be an effective witness for God in the life of others. Never underestimate your testimony, the power of the unique story of your life. It will give hope to those who are hopeless, direction to those who are unknowingly lost and also remind you, each time you tell it, of all that God has done in your life.

It's time to start to tell your story; it's time to say, 'IAMREDEMPTION. Here is the story of what God did for me.'

IAMREDEMP†ION.org STORIES

Broken free from gambling

I was in a troubled, sad time in my life, desperately searching for someone or something. My marriage had fallen apart when my wife left me. On reflection I see now that she realised that life without me would be better; we had financial difficulties, massive debts that were mainly due to my gambling problem, which she was not fully aware of. I never had any money, and we had never even spoken about having a family. That was around 2005.

Then I met a friend at work (who would later become my wife!). We got talking about life and making wrong choices. So much of what she said made sense. I asked her why she thought this way and she told me about God.

Not long later I went to church for the first time, and ended up giving my life to God. Fast forward to now, and I am a living story of redemption. I have my own home, I am free from my gambling addiction, I have a fantastic wife, two beautiful kids and a great family.

More than all of this, though, I have hope, confidence and security. I can't imagine my life without God; all I know is, it wouldn't be good! I have been promoted twice at work since beginning my relationship with God, and right now I believe God is preparing me for life outside the Armed Forces. I am extremely excited about what He wants to do through me, our church and my family and friends.

Graham

CHAPTER FOUR

CARRIERS OF THE REDEMPTIVE HEART OF GOD

Is this not the fast that I have chosen: to loose the bonds of wickedness, to undo the heavy burdens, to let the oppressed go free, and that you break every yoke? Is it not to share your bread with the hungry, and that you bring to your house the poor who are cast out; when you see the naked, that you cover him, and not hide yourself from your own flesh? Then your light shall break forth like the morning, your healing shall spring forth speedily, and your righteousness shall go before you; the glory of the LORD shall be your rear guard.

Isaiah 58:6-8

et's look now at the second edge to the mandate and call of IAMREDEMPTION. It's a call for people to not just tell others about what God has done in redeeming them, but to also make the decision that they are going to allow God to use their life to be involved in a redemption outbreak in the life of another.

As we have already stated, Jesus is the 'I AM' to IAMREDEMPTION, but when it comes to manifesting His redemptive intentions in the lives of others, He desires for us to be His hands and feet. It's good that we allow Him to use our mouth, but He also often needs to use of the rest of us. When we make the decision to be redeemed people that tell our story, it is an awesome thing. We become display boards for the endless possibilities of what God can do in a person's life. But we need to remember that God also desires us to be His delivery men and workmen that carry His redemptive heart, intention and potential into the everyday lives of others whether that is an individual in need or a whole community.

When we pray for redemption in a person's life or in the life of a community, do we ever realise that possibly we are the answer to that prayer? God also needs a people that will turn up and, in His name, become the redemption in the lives of others. Are we willing to not just preach at others, but also to practically roll up our sleeves and spend some of our time and energy to see those lives redeemed and brought in accordance with God's desires?

REDEMPTION ALWAYS HAS A COST

If we truly want to see redemption in the lives of others we need to understand that it always has a cost; someone always has to pay or give something to see another redeemed. Whether it be a payment of time, energy or money, there is always a cost to redemption. It becomes nothing more than a nice prayer if people pray for redemption in the life of another, yet have no intention of giving anything to make it happen. Sometimes we may not be a part of the answer, but we need to have our hearts ready and willing to be if needed.

Remember our own redemption (being purchased back to God), cost the Father the very best of what He had, His only son Jesus. Though He would be raised from the dead on the third day, the torment He had to witness upon His son during our Lord's sacrifice was more than the human mind can conceive. When we consider what they did to Jesus both leading up to the cross and on the cross, we certainly become aware that our redemption did not by any means come cheap.

> Knowing that you were not redeemed with corruptible things, like silver or gold, from your aimless conduct received by tradition from your fathers, but with the precious blood of Christ, as of a lamb without blemish and without spot.
>
> **1 Peter 1:18-19**

In the same way, we need to always be ready and willing to lay down our lives and pay the cost to see God's redemptive intentions come into being in the lives of others. A great example of this is found in the account of the Good Samaritan in Luke 10. Let's take a closer look at what Jesus taught as He answered the question 'who is my neighbour?' that was given him by a lawyer that day.

> Then Jesus answered and said: 'A certain man went down from Jerusalem to Jericho, and fell among thieves, who stripped him of his clothing, wounded him, and departed, leaving him half dead. Now by chance a certain priest came down that road. And when he saw him, he passed by on the other side. Likewise a Levite, when he arrived at the place, came and looked, and passed by on the other side. But a certain Samaritan, as he journeyed, came where he was. And when he saw him, he had compassion. So he went to him and bandaged his wounds, pouring on oil and wine; and he set him on

his own animal, brought him to an inn, and took care of him. On the next day, when he departed, he took out two denarii, gave them to the innkeeper, and said to him, "Take care of him; and whatever more you spend, when I come again, I will repay you." So which of these three do you think was neighbour to him who fell among the thieves?' And he said, 'He who showed mercy on him.' Then Jesus said to him, 'Go and do likewise.'

Luke 10:30-37

There are three men in this account: two that represent religious men and one a Samaritan. Being a Samaritan, he represented the one who should have been least likely to help. Notice how those who represented religion crossed the street when they encountered a man who had been robbed and was desperately in need of someone to be IAMREDEMPTION in his life. But then the Samaritan came by, the least likely one, who, in the minds of the people of that day, should have been in the queue behind the other two. He discovers the man who has been left half dead and instantly steps into the situation and takes responsibility for the well-being of this poor soul. It wasn't his problem; he didn't know this man. The incredible thing that separated him from the other two was though it may not have been his problem, he made it his responsibility. That is what IAMREDEMPTION does. It steps into situations that have not been caused or created by you and it spends itself to bring a change of story in the life of those in need.

After stepping in to take responsibility, we get a lovely

picture of how the Samaritan man devotes himself to this helpless person. He spends his energy, his time and his money to make sure that the man is positioned in a place of recovery and is set up for a better ending to the story of what had happened to him. He makes sure he is safe, and then underwrites what the man needs before moving on to where he was actually going. Notice he even says, 'I will come back and check on him.' That is commitment to a long-term responsibility; he never settled for a short-term fix.

At this point in the narrative, Jesus throws out a very blunt question and challenge to the lawyer and others who were listening. 'Who did right to his neighbour?' His last response after they answered was the very mandate of IAMREDEMPTION: 'Now go and do the same.' I believe He still says that to us today and this remains our commission when you find or stumble across a need – do what you can to help the person – don't cross over the road or close your heart to it.

REDEMPTIVE PATHWAYS

We are commissioned to be God's redemptive pathway. We need to allow Him to use our lives to be the pathways between a God who adores humanity and the humanity that has had Him misrepresented to them. If we are willing, God will use our lives to join Him and the people that need Him back together. Most people who need redemption will rarely read a Bible or go to church, but they will read *you* as they rub shoulders with you daily. Let us never act or speak in such a way that it makes people not want to know the God that we profess. Rather, let the way we live awaken intrigue and curiosity towards God, the One we say has changed the story of our lives. When we get involved and spend ourselves for those in need to make their lives better, we lay a pathway to God. When we dare to be IAMREDEMPTION in the lives of those who have been robbed, abused and destroyed, we lay an open pathway for them to want to listen to our testimony and meet the One that changed our storyline. In the natural, workmen will lay a pathway from one place to another. Whether it is concrete or tarmac, they put down the material to create a pathway from point A to point B. Our lives are the material that God needs to daily lay down so others can journey back to Him. Let us be as the disciples of old, people who are daily willing to lay down our lives for others.

> Greater love has no one than this, than to lay down one's life for his friends.
>
> **John 15:13**

> By this we know love, because He laid down His life for us. And we also ought to lay down our lives for the brethren.
>
> **1 John 3:16**

REDEMPTIVE INTERRUPTIONS

We are also God's redemptive interruptions. God wants to use our lives to cause divine interruptions in the lives of others.

He does this so He can redeem them and re-route their lives to a better destination and future. As we have said before, every person has a story to their life and is presently living out the manuscript of it. Most are no different than what we were previously, going aimlessly and ignorantly in a direction without seeing the consequences ahead. Lives that are heading for destruction, breakdown or loss both of life in regard to their eternity, and also in the life they experience here on Earth. Think about it, what happened in your life? God sent a redemptive interruption and most often it came in the form of a person. Someone entered the storyline at a crucial time and introduced you to Jesus and His intentions for your life. Because of their part, your life was then re-routed and things began to change as divine new direction came. Imagine where you may be today if God never sent you that redemptive interruption at the right moment? Now it's simply time for you to be His interruption in the storyline of another. Right now, outside your front door, people are heading for the edge of a cliff and they don't know it. Their marriages are falling apart, families are disintegrating and they are unaware. They are dabbling with things that could have terrible life-shaping ramifications and, worst of all, if they don't know Jesus they are one breath away from spending an eternity in torment. God sees them and has redemptive plans for them, but needs a physical interruption to reach out and re-route them. That's where we come in: we are His redemptive interruptions!

It's a very powerful thing indeed to think that God has

entrusted us with the power to carry His redemptive intent into the lives of others. He wants to use us to cause a new direction or plot change in the manuscript of people's lives. How could that not excite you? He wants to drop you into the confused and broken storyline of other people, knowing that your life will be the interruption that is needed to cause an outbreak of redemption in their life.

WILL YOU CARRY HIS REDEMPTIVE HEART?

If you have ever been around me for any amount of time, you will know that one of my signature messages is called 'The Day of the Donkey'. This message has constantly resurfaced throughout my time in ministry, even finding its way into the pages of my book, *God's Blueprint for His Church* [1]. In writing *IAMREDEMPTION*, I sense it is another great opportunity to look at this simple account of a donkey freed for a purpose.

> After Jesus had said this, he went on ahead, going up to Jerusalem. As he approached Bethphage and Bethany at the hill called the Mount of Olives, he sent two of his disciples, saying to them, 'Go to the village ahead of you, and as you enter it, you will find a colt tied there, which no one has ever ridden. Untie it and bring it here. If anyone asks you, "Why are you untying it?" say, "The Lord needs it."' Those who were sent ahead

---

1. *God's Blueprint for His Church*. Elmes, Andy. Great Big Life Publishing, ISBN 978-0-9928027-2-1

went and found it just as he had told them. As they were
untying the colt, its owners asked them, 'Why are you
untying the colt?' They replied, 'The Lord needs it.'
Luke 19:28-34 (NIV)

In this account, two of Jesus' team were sent to a village to
free a donkey that was tied to a pole. The donkey obviously
belonged to someone because Jesus pre-warned them how
to respond if they were confronted as they helped themselves
to the donkey. And confronted they were, as they untied this
beast of burden. The man must have shouted at them exclaiming,
'Excuse me, what are you doing with my donkey?' in pretty
much the same manner you would if you saw two men
getting ready to drive away in your car. At that moment, one
of the disciples does as he was told and pulls out the statement
he had been given by Jesus in case a confrontation like this
took place. The statement that said, 'It's OK, the Lord needs
it.' That declaration must have felt very flimsy when you are
holding the rope of another person's donkey! But to the
disciples' relief, the man heard, smiled and sent the disciples
on their way. In further thinking about this, I presume it was
a pre-arranged deal – maybe Jesus had blessed his family at
one time and the man had said something to the effect that
if He ever needed to borrow his ride, He could help Himself.

Next, the disciples bring the donkey to Jesus and He is
then seated on it and led into Jerusalem, the most significant
city of its time. Think about what happened here from the

donkey's perspective. The donkey started the day tied to a pole. Usually his day was spent walking around in endless circles; it had only ever known captivity, so never knew what freedom would look like in comparison.

But this day, it all changed. The messengers of God arrived, loosed it from captivity and brought it to Jesus. Did Jesus loose him because He had a soft spot in His heart for donkeys? Did He want to release this poor donkey into a donkey sanctuary He had set up on a green hill far away? No, He set the donkey free because He had a purpose for it. That purpose was to carry Him where He needed to go. Let's now compare our lives to that donkey for a moment. We are of greater worth than a donkey, of course, yet the story has some basic similarities. Like that animal, we were bound. I don't know about you, but when Jesus came to set me free I was bound up, messed up, addicted and confused. I was going around in circles just like that donkey, fooling myself that I was heading somewhere when I was actually going nowhere real fast. But Jesus sent His word and liberated my life. He untied me and set me free; for that I am eternally grateful. To be free would be enough to warrant me praising and serving Him all of my days because as the Bible says, he who is forgiven much loves much (Luke 7:47). But what amazes me most is that not only did He free me but, like that colt, He had a purpose for me, too. Not a purpose that would make me a slave, rather a purpose that would make me an ambassador (2 Corinthians 5:20).

We have been freed for a purpose, a purpose that would impact the lives of others. (For a more detailed explanation of this truth get a copy of my book *God's Blueprint for His Church* and study the chapter called, 'Created By, Created For').

So what purpose did the donkey have? It had the privilege of carrying Jesus where He wanted to go next. Now consider this for a moment – who or what was Jesus? We know that Jesus, among other things, was God's only beloved Son and Saviour of the world. But think about it, Jesus was also God's redemptive heart personified! He was God's redemptive heart made flesh, sent to dwell among us. You see, God has always had a redemptive heart for man, but man lost the understanding of that. Religion, with all its layers and masquerades, had separated man from the revelation that God's heart was one of redemption. God had to unveil His heart again to man and that's what He did in His Son. Jesus was an exact reflection of His Father and representation of His Father's heart; a heart of redemption.

> [He] has in these last days spoken to us by His Son, whom He has appointed heir of all things, through whom also He made the worlds; **who being the brightness of His glory and the express image of His person, and upholding all things by the word of His power**, when He had by Himself purged our sins, sat down at the right hand of the Majesty on high.
>
> **Hebrews 1:2-3**

I like how it says in *The Message* translation, *'This Son perfectly mirrors God, and is stamped with God's nature.'*

What does this mean? Simply that if two thousand years ago, you encountered Jesus walking down the road, then you also encountered the Father. Everything you needed to know about God the Father and His character, you could learn from watching His Son. Jesus put this so well in a conversation He had with Philip.

> Jesus said to him, 'Have I been with you so long, and yet you have not known Me, Philip? **He who has seen Me has seen the Father**; so how can you say, "Show us the Father"?'
>
> **John 14:9**

So Jesus was a physical manifestation of the heart and nature of God on the earth. Watch carefully what Jesus did while on the earth and you see the intentions of the Father Heart of God for humanity being performed and outworked on a daily basis. Think about that, everywhere Jesus went on that donkey, redemption broke out. Lives were restored, healed, put back together again because that is God's heart – to give life. As it says in John 10:10, the devil is the one who comes to kill, steal and destroy people; Jesus has come to bring life, new beginnings, fresh hope and restoration to our tomorrows. Everywhere Jesus went, the redemptive heart of God broke out and lives were impacted and radically changed.

If that donkey could tell of what he saw, imagine the stories! Here is my point again about comparing us to that donkey. The privilege he had was that he got to carry the redemptive heart of God (Jesus) into the worlds of others, so that God's redemptive intentions for man could be released in the lives of those in need. We now have that privilege, we now have the honour of carrying the redemptive heart of God into the lives of others, whether it is individuals or communities. God wants to use our everyday lives to carry and bring His redemptive intentions to the worlds of others.

So the question is, will you bear your back to Christ the redeemer? It was for freedom that Christ has set you free (Galatians 5:1). You need to understand He also has a purpose for your freed life, that purpose is the saving and redemption of other people.

Whenever I preach on the donkey, I always end the message by taking an offering. When I say that, people normally think I am going to target their money and prepare for the invasion. I shock them by telling them that God is not just after their money – He is after their life! I then inform them that the offering I intend to take is a donkey offering. We are going to give you the opportunity to put your life in an offering for God to use. As people choose to do this, they are saying to God, 'Thank You for giving me my freedom, for untying me from what held me, including the grip of sin and death. Now, I give my freed life back to You to use as You need it. Let my life be Your donkey, use my life to carry

Your redemptive heart wherever it needs to go.'

I am aware that we are not in a meeting together today and you're reading a book, but I want to challenge you with that same challenge. Will you give your life to God in a donkey offering today? Why not join the thousands of others who have responded to this offering over the years and pray this very simple prayer:

> Thank You, Jesus, for liberating my life from the captivity that once held it. Thank You for untying me from my pole. You have given me freedom as a gift, but now I want to give it back to You. Let my life be a donkey for Your purposes. Let my life from this day, in a greater way, carry Your redemptive heart into the lives of others.
>
> **Amen.**

When we allow God to use our lives, we become very powerful vessels indeed. When His redemptive heart is carried in us, we find opportunities to be a miracle or a blessing in the lives of others. Just as redemption broke out everywhere Jesus went, so it will break out wherever you go. Be expectant, because it was Jesus that said, 'Greater things will you do.'

> Very truly I tell you, whoever believes in me will do the works I have been doing, and they will do even greater things than these, because I am going to the Father.
>
> **John 14:12 (NIV)**

God desperately wants to use your life to see the storylines of others radically changed, whether it is in a person, community or even a city. If you will dare to be IAMREDEMPTION in the lives of others, watch what starts to happen through your life. I am so grateful to have been involved in countless incredible story-changes in the lives of people over the years. Let me encourage you with a couple of stories of what happened to me some months ago with a community and a very special person.

CHANGING COMMUNITIES

I had been ministering with my oldest daughter, Olivia, in a remote region in Philippines. I had the privilege to hold a Bible study in a small farming village that made its livelihood from growing sugar cane. We had gone off-road to visit this small village and I was delighted to be given the opportunity to speak. As I preached through my translator, I spoke a very simple message about redemption. In fact, it was pretty much the story I told you in chapter two about the man who made a ship from matchsticks. I told them of God's redemptive love for them and then gave them the opportunity to make Him their friend. I was overjoyed when the majority of the people responded in the makeshift meeting hall made out of sugar canes. I was able to lead them into salvation and relationship with Him.

As we happily left the village, so grateful for all God had done, I looked back and saw that the name of the village was called St Andréas. I turned and asked my pastor friend, 'What does that mean?'

I had to laugh when he said, 'Saint Andy's'. Surely God had a sense of humour, a little farming village literally in the middle of nowhere – a village called St Andy's! I remember thinking to myself that God must surely have further plans for us here in the future. Little did I know what was coming. It was only a week later that typhoon Haiyan hit and as with many villages in that area, most of St Andréas was totally flattened.

I was only just back in the UK when I heard the news, and I was heartbroken. I had led these people into spiritual redemption, but now they had nowhere safe to live, no fresh water or supplies. Straight away I knew what I had to do. The next day was Sunday and I spoke to our church about what had happened and said to them, 'We have brought them redemption spiritually, now God wants to use us to bring redemption to them practically. We have to let them understand that God cares about their present day lives, not just their eternity.' A spontaneous offering was taken and enough money received to buy them generators, food supplies and materials to make temporary shelters. But through the giving of the church and other friends, we raised more than enough to do what we initially planned. I began to think about what would happen when the storms returned again. So we expanded our vision and decided to replace the cane buildings they lived in with some permanent concrete ones, giving them a safe place long term and not just for the moment. It was amazing to see the church and friends get behind this as we purposed we would not just pray for them, but be God's arms, legs and wallets, too. That we would stand up for them in their time of need and say IAMREDEMPTION.

As I write this, building has already begun on the first four-family home in St Andy's. We are planning on constructing more units to help restore that village, as well as in other areas and villages similar to that one. Since then, we have also started another project of redemption that involves setting up a sewing industry to help change the economy of the village. In this place, as with many others, they survive on farming sugar cane. There is no other way of making income apart from selling a few animals. The trouble with farming sugar cane, however, is that there are five months of the year where you are not working with crops and so any profit you made is eaten up in surviving. I spoke to my friend Miriam in the village and we came up with this sewing plan. If we could get machines there and train some of the farmers to sew, we could create new industry that could create income for the village and help it see a transformation.

So that's what we did. I talked to a few friends and was able to get our first four, heavy duty professional sewing machines purchased. Big thanks to our Family Church pastor in the Philippines, Rhic, who sourced them in Manila and shipped them to the village. The machines are now there, training has been accomplished and a new industry has begun in the village that was formally hopeless. Something you may ask is, how could something so practical be redemption – is that really what redemption is? Absolutely! What do you suppose God wanted to do when He saw their situation? I believe He wanted to create something that would redeem the lives of the people in that village. He had a redemptive plan; He just needed a group of people to physically make it happen. Some people who would declare, IAMREDEMPTION in that situation. You see, God wants us to carry the message of His eternal redemption to others, but He also wants us to be redemption for Him in their practical lives as well. When we are faced with an opportunity to turn people's lives around for them, we need to jump in with both feet.

If you are saying 'but what can just one person do?' then remember what I did in the above account: I found some friends, and talked to the church. What we achieved really was a 'we are redemption' project that brought a lot of change to the lives of many. So, who could you work with? When two or more people who carry the heart of IAMREDEMPTION find each other and join together it is a very powerful thing. As it is often quoted, 'one can put a thousand to flight but two ten thousand'. That describes the power of synergy. When people work together in unity, they produce an output that is greater than the single parts involved can produce on their own. This is why the devil works so hard to keep the people that would work really well together apart, because he knows together they can solve ten thousand problems verses just a thousand each. That's why I'm believing for an

IAMREDEMPTION army. Imagine the difference we can create in the lives of others if we found each other and pooled our strength, resources and ability?

Let's face it, it would have been a lot less hassle and a lot cheaper to 'cross the street' like the priest and the Levite when I was safely back in my own country, but that's not what we are called to do, is it?

This is just one account of the difference we were able to make in a small village thousands of miles away. I told it with the purpose of inspiring you to do the same. You see, the reality is that need is not just in villages on the other side of the world; it is actually all around us wherever we are. If you are looking for need, you will always find it, believe me. I am so very proud of our community outreach teams in Family Church that work fifty-two weeks a year to bring redemptive change to the lives of others. A couple of years ago, God really touched many of our hearts again with the great commission and the call to go. As a result of this we launched many initiatives in our local communities that carried God's redemptive heart into very needy situations. I stand constantly amazed at the commitment of the teams that run the food banks, minister to the homeless, turn up in our housing estates to put on kids' programmes and sometimes just pick up rubbish. The love and passion of these people have truly turned the heads of our community towards us as a church and, more importantly, back to a loving God. Through their sacrificial giving they are constantly reintroducing people back to Him.

I could boast in so many ways of our people and different teams that have committed to be IAMREDEMPTION in the lives of others and am so excited that we have, in many ways, only just begun.

What projects and teams does your church have to carry God's redemptive heart to others? Why not sign up to be on a team, or ask what you can practically do or give to make what they do more effective. As you do, you are standing up to say IAMREDEMPTION in the lives of others, people that God adores.

CHANGING PEOPLE'S STORIES

God giving us the ability to re-route a person's life became very real to me once again on that last trip to Philippines when I met a certain young lady. To protect her identity, we will call her Sara. God used this little lady to show me the difference we can make in a person's life if we will dare to step forward and say IAMREDEMPTION.

It was when I was leaving St Andréas (St Andy's) that I first met Sara. She looked like such a little girl as she sat on the back of the truck we were travelling in. We had put plastic chairs from the church in the back of a pickup truck to get us all to the village and were all laughing as we fell all over the place, jostling over the numerous bumps on the mud track road. Sara sat quietly in the corner as we trekked on and, for some reason, my attention was drawn to her. I could feel God prompting me, but was trying to work out why. She looked about nine and I assumed she was the daughter of the lady driving the truck (assumption can be such a dangerous thing). But there was something about this girl that struck me. Perhaps it was that she looked like one of my own daughters but, no, it was more than that. It was as if God was speaking one word over her as I looked at her that day: REDEMPTION.

I was travelling with my daughter Olivia and with Rhic, who is our pastor in the Philippines. I started to share with them that God was prompting my heart about this girl. I asked Rhic to talk to her in her language and find out more about her, which he did. After a long dialogue, Rhic turned to me and started to explain. Her name was Sara, the lady driving the truck was not her mum, just one who had been concerned for her. She saw her run into the sugar cane fields one night after working on the farm. Afraid she would be hurt, and prompted by God, she took her in and had been watching over her for a week or so. It turned out that most of my assumptions about Sara were wrong. She was actually sixteen, not nine, but was malnourished and had many times just eaten sugar cane because she had nothing else to eat. Her mother had died when she was nine; her dad was a drunk who beat her and sent her out to earn money for him to buy more drink. Without going into too much detail, village life had been brutal to her and taken away every dream she had as a child. Through Rhic, I asked her about her childhood dreams. She looked down and said that she had dreamed of being a teacher, but her dad had taken those dreams away by sending her to work the fields. I asked Rhic what would become of her. He told me that she would more than likely come to harm in the field, become pregnant, marry the wrong person to get away from her father, but never leave the village or live out her dreams. She was not alone; there were so many other girls in the villages around that area and throughout the rural regions of the Philippines that could pretty much tell the same story, if not worse. But this moment was about this girl – God was challenging me and it was to do with her redemption. It was at that moment, sitting in the back of a pickup truck, that I heard God say to me, 'What are you going to do about it?'

I suddenly realised that God was not physically coming to help her re-write her life. He had sent me as his envoy or representative; it was now my responsibility to be His redemptive interruption in her life. He wanted me to step in and get involved and not 'cross the street'.

I remember talking to God in my heart, as I sat there wrestling with various emotions. I remember saying, 'God, this is not fair. I don't know her. What I can do? I am on a plane in two days and I live in the UK!' Then I heard myself speak to Rhic and say, 'This is not acceptable. I want to help.' I heard myself carry on, 'I want to put her in a safe home, I want to take her from her father and get her educated, so she has the future she dreamed.' I could not believe what was coming out of my mouth but, to be honest, I loved it! It was right; because I knew it was God's heart for her!

Once again, I stood up in my life and said, 'IAMREDEMPTION'. That afternoon was amazing – surely God was involved as we accomplished so much in such a little time. Miriam, the driver, agreed to take her in permanently and raise her like a daughter. She had fallen in love with her, and had been praying days before because she did not know how she could provide for her. We arranged it that day that Sara never had to go home again or be hurt by her abusive father. We found some people to help her get the education she needed to start school. The pastor and his wife who were with us agreed to take responsibility for her and to teach her the things of God and help her to know Jesus for herself. We arranged that support would come from my family and me to give her all she needed. That day, Olivia and I adopted another daughter to our family! That night I called my wife, Gina, and told her about Sara. Gina wanted me to put her in my suitcase and bring her home! Of course, we couldn't do that but, with Miriam's help, we could be like a mum and dad from afar. We could provide what she needed to make those dreams she once had come true.

Even though she couldn't understand a word we said to her, we fell in love with her instantly and made sure that, when we left, she was safe, taken care of and would be treated like she was one of our kids. The icing on the cake came for me that night; I was preaching in a church near the village, and Sara came with Miriam and sat with Olivia. She listened to my message as it was translated, and when I made an appeal for salvation, I saw her little hand go up.

Why am I telling this personal story? Because I want you to see that if we dare to stand up when we find need, God will use us to be His redemption plan in the lives of others. That day, the storyline of that little girl's life changed. Her life was re-routed by God through me. A story was radically changed, a new direction established. Sara was one little girl from an unknown village, but she was a girl who caused my heart to come alive again to the fact that God has given us the power and authority to change the stories of people's lives on His behalf. And the reality is, you don't need to go to a village in the middle of nowhere to find a need that you can intervene in. They are all around – people living stories that desperately need changing. Will you be a story-changer for God? Will you be the Good Samaritan in the life of another? Will you be IAMREDEMPTION?

This storyline actually has continued as, after meeting Sara, we also met her friend who had an equally horrific story. She was sixteen and had had her first child at twelve by an uncle, and her second child by another uncle when she was fourteen. We met other little girls who had similar tragedies, and I knew this was going to become a bigger redemptive plan than I thought. We are now looking to open, through IAMREDEMPTION – THE FUND, a home for some of these girls. Our dream is to take them into a home called the Father's House, to care for them, educate them and see their lives re-routed in the direction of what God has for them.

If you are looking for need, you will always find it. The question is, are you looking?

'When the Son of Man comes in His glory, and all the holy angels with Him, then He will sit on the throne of His glory. All the nations will be gathered before Him, and He will separate them one from another, as a shepherd divides his sheep from the goats. And He will set the sheep on His right hand, but the goats on the left. Then the King will say to those on His right hand, "Come, you blessed of My Father, inherit the kingdom prepared for you from the foundation of the world: for I was hungry and you gave Me food; I was thirsty and you gave Me drink; I was a stranger and you took Me in; I was naked and you clothed Me; I was sick and you visited Me; I was in prison and you came to Me." Then the righteous will answer Him, saying, "Lord, when did we see You hungry and feed You, or thirsty and give You drink? When did we see You a stranger and take You in, or naked and clothe You?"

And the King will answer and say to them, "Assuredly, I say to you, inasmuch as you did it to one of the least of these My brethren, you did it to Me." Then He will also say to those on the left hand, "Depart from Me, you cursed, into the everlasting fire prepared for the devil and his angels: for I was hungry and you gave Me no food; I was thirsty and you gave Me no drink; I was a stranger and you did not take Me in, naked and you did not clothe Me, sick and in prison and you did not visit Me." Then they also will answer Him, saying, "Lord, when did we see You hungry or thirsty or a stranger or naked or sick or in prison, and did not minister to You?" Then He will answer them, saying, "Assuredly, I say to you, inasmuch as you did not do it to one of the least of these, you did not do it to Me."'

Matthew 25:31-38, 40-45

IAMREDEMP†ION.org STORIES

Living life with a new purpose

The day I let Jesus into my life was the day I started the best friendship of all time. I was overwhelmed by the force of it. I had no idea how much my life would change that day. A good friend of mine invited me to church. She didn't once quote scripture to me and, in fact, we didn't talk about God much at all.

I was such an angry person; not to others, but how I felt inside. I was always thinking – is this it! A violent relationship and one marriage behind me, I met a really loving man. At last, I had found my soul mate. We got married, and started a family.

Then things started to look black, everything turned on its head. I had just had my second baby. Both my parents were terminally ill. I had been caring for them, a busy toddler and a new baby. Cracks were starting to show. In quick succession, my son nearly died, my dad died, then my mum. I could feel myself falling faster than I could cry out for help, and no-one could catch me. I was hearing voices and planning my death. It felt to me like it really was the best thing for everyone if I wasn't around.

I spent 5 months in a psychiatric unit. Everything changed: a part of me was lost. When I met my friend I was still on medication, and it all seemed so pointless. I was ready to be saved. It was amazing! I felt like I had come home. God grabbed me and said, "I will never let you go". I could feel His strength, His love and His peace all over me.

My life is so amazing. I have a God who cares deeply about ME. I am not saying that bad stuff doesn't happen, but I don't need to go through it alone. I am living my life with a new purpose. It's hard to explain the changes that happen inside of you. It's like having a new you, a complete, fresh start.

Di

CHAPTER FIVE

A REDEMPTION ARMY

> And they sang a new song, saying: 'You are worthy to take the scroll, and to open its seals; for You were slain, and have redeemed us to God by Your blood out of every tribe and tongue and people and nation.'
>
> **Revelation 5:9**

I hear an army rising up, a Redemption Army.

They are rising up from every walk of life and church denomination; a people whose hearts have been marked by the redemptive heart of God. They have counted the cost and made their decision to live beyond the boundaries of their own existence for the benefit of others. They can no longer settle for just sitting comfortably in church but are on their feet, poised and ready to go, fuelled by a desire to carry the heartbeat of God into their communities and the needy worlds that surround their everyday lives. They are ready and willing to lay down whatever holds them back to see redemption break out in the lives of others. Believing for open doors, they seek to impact individuals and communities, to be God's hands and feet to the orphan, the widow and all those in need, to walk the corridors of prisons and districts that the feet of the church have not been for far too long.

They need not a uniform or rank, and have found their marching orders in the presence of their Lord. The commission given by Christ two thousand years ago has become personal and they take it seriously. Aware of the time we are in and need that is so very present, they tirelessly give of themselves again and again to see redemption break out.

This is no mere gathering of contented saints, another project or business as usual. This is a marching army of people, stirred to their innermost being by the redemptive heart of God for man. They need no applause or affirmation because they are not doing what they do to be seen by men. The only accreditation they desire is to one day hear those words when they stand before the God of all redemption, 'Well done, good and faithful servant.'

Don't you want to be a part of such an army?

INSPIRED BY WHAT GOD HAS DONE BEFORE

When it comes to heroes in modern church history, one of my favourites is William Booth, the founder of the Salvation Army which is indeed a worldwide army of people who place great passion and importance on carrying the salvation message of God both in word and deed to those who need it, whether that need be spiritual or humanitarian. In studying the origins of the Salvation Army, I was inspired by what possessed the heart of a London preacher called William Booth. I believe that the redemptive heart of God was burning in him just as it is again setting fire in the hearts of many today. Listen to the agenda of God in this account of its early days:

The Salvation Army began in 1865 when William Booth, a London minister, gave up the comfort of his pulpit and decided to take his message into the streets where it would reach the poor, the homeless, the hungry and the destitute.

His original aim was to send converts to established churches of the day, but soon he realised that the poor did not feel comfortable or welcome in the pews of most of the churches and chapels of Victorian England. Regular churchgoers were appalled when these shabbily dressed, unwashed people came to join them in worship. Booth decided to found a church especially for them – the East London Christian Mission. The mission grew slowly, but Booth's faith in God remained undiminished.

In May 1878, Booth summoned his son, Bramwell, and his good friend George Railton to read a proof of the Christian Mission's annual report. At the top it read: THE CHRISTIAN MISSION is A VOLUNTEER ARMY. Bramwell strongly objected to this wording. He was not a volunteer: he was compelled to do God's work. So, in a flash of inspiration, Booth crossed out 'Volunteer' and wrote 'Salvation'. The Salvation Army was born. (excerpt taken from salvationarmy.org [1])

———————————

I believe that this is happening again, but not through one group of people or one specific denomination, but rather across the body of Christ as a whole. In many ways God's church is awakening and rising up again to walk alongside these salvation soldiers, who for many years have laboured to see redemption in the lives of others. But in another way, it's a

---

1. http://www.salvationarmy.org/ihq/history

new thing that excludes none and includes all. It's not in any means a replacement of something, but rather a joining together for a common godly purpose. I honour William Booth and the ministry of the Salvation Army with everything that I am. But I sense an even bigger army rising; an army of people redeemed from every tribe and tongue; an army that marches in unison with the common mandate to love God and love people. I'm not talking about something that replaces any former army but that complements it. We will walk shoulder to shoulder to be one relentless, unstoppable new army with one king and one calling: the redemption and salvation of man.

PEOPLE WHO WILL GLADLY SPEND THE CURRENCY OF THEIR LIFE ON OTHERS

This army is made up of people who have considered the currency of their days and purposed to spend it on the redemption of others. You see, the greatest currency a person possesses is not found in a bank or building society – it is the days, months and years of the life you have left to live. All other commodities mean nothing in comparison to the worth and potential of the days of your life. Think about it. What profit is every other type of wealth if your life was to cease? The breath in our lungs and the pulse in our body remain the greatest currency that we possess. May we choose to both respect it and spend it wisely.

When we speak of redeeming things, we need to remember that the Bible actually speaks of us redeeming our time. I believe when it speaks of the redemption of our time it is referring to using it for things of eternal worth that benefit the lives of others.

> See then that you walk circumspectly, not as fools but as wise, **redeeming the time, because the days are evil.** Therefore do not be unwise, but understand what the will of the Lord is.
>
> **Ephesians 5:15-17**

Look now at this passage of scripture from *The Message* translation. Again it brings out its meaning well:

> Don't waste your time on useless work, mere busywork, the barren pursuits of darkness. Expose these things for the sham they are. It's a scandal when people waste their lives on things they must do in the darkness where no one will see. Rip the cover off those frauds and see how attractive they look in the light of Christ. Wake up from your sleep, climb out of your coffins; Christ will show you the light! So watch your step. Use your head. Make the most of every chance you get. These are desperate times! Don't live carelessly, unthinkingly. Make sure you understand what the Master wants.
>
> **Ephesians 5:15-17 (The Message)**

What does it look like to redeem the time or spend the currency of your life wisely? I believe firstly it is to have spent it in knowing God and living out His will for your life, but also it's to have spent it in enriching the lives of others. In heaven there will be no golf trophies, shiny cars or investment portfolios. Your trophies will be the lives that the time you spent on the earth had an effect upon. Many who have lived only for themselves will one day be very surprised when they open their eyes in another life to realise that everything they strived to attain achieved nothing in the light of their eternal existence. On the other hand, the person who seemed to have nothing but faithfully lived for God and the well-being of others will dance in the fields of great inheritance as they are surrounded by people whose lives were changed or impacted by the selfless life they chose to live.

SEVENTEEN GOLD COINS

Your life truly is the greatest currency you possess, so purpose to spend it wisely. I remember last year, we moved into our new offices and I was considering what ornament I would like on my desk to motivate me to live well. Someone suggested an eagle, because every pastor has an eagle, right? Did I need further encouragement to fly or soar higher? No, not really. Someone else suggested a set of scales so that I would be reminded to hold all things in correct balance. Certainly earlier in ministry this was much needed as I did not understand balancing things as well as I do now.

No, what I wanted on my desk to motivate me to live my best life was a lot simpler and less ornate than a golden eagle or a set of brass scales. All I needed was seventeen gold coins (pound coins). You see I have discovered the secret of the currency of my days and have realised that each remaining year of my life is in fact the greatest currency I have to spend and to wisely invest. You see, the years of our life are just like coins in a bag:

we are all given an amount to spend. No one knows exactly how many a person may have except for God, but we all have some. When we are young, we don't think about the remaining years as much as we should because the bag seems so heavy with coins. But then you start to get older and you notice the bag getting lighter. As you begin to hit middle age, you become internally conscious that the bag is nearly half empty now. This, I believe, should cause a greater appreciation for the ones that remain rather than regret for the ones that are gone. This is, in fact, a hallmark of a life that is being lived well. When the bag begins to get lighter, the value of what remains suddenly begins to increase. Remember, there are no refunds for the coins that have been spent, but there should be God-inspired purpose-driven plans for the ones that are left. What are you doing when you do this? We are doing what the Bible instructs us to do: we are numbering our days, numbering them not with fear or feelings of regret, but rather from a heart of wisdom.

> So teach us to number our days, that we may gain a heart of wisdom.
>
> **Psalm 90:12**

It's often around the halfway mark that people make seemingly sudden radical decisions concerning how they will spend the remaining currency of their life. For those are foolish or unwise, they often buy into the midlife crisis deception and do something stupid like change their wife or buy a sports car or speed boat. Or they embark on some pointless endeavour in a desperate bid to regain something they think they lost or were robbed of. Others who have a wiser heart don't enter the deceptive courts of mid-life crisis, but rather the realm of mid-life re-purpose. For them it is often the moment they stop living to just earn money to get more things, and instead will get involved in a humanitarian project. This is exactly what happened when we see the Microsoft genius billionaire suddenly leave his job and go to work with water projects or aids relief in the Developing World. People they worked with are often surprised and ask why did they suddenly do that? I think it's because they had been internally weighing the currency of their days and a realisation had risen up within them which said, 'I don't want to spend what is left of my life on what I spent the first half on.'

It is rarely a quick or spontaneous decision, though it often just looks that way to people outside of their life. But, in reality, it was a growing realisation within them that had been present and ever strengthening over many months if not years.

Outside of this type of midlife turn around, we all need to consider the realities of our life being the greatest currency we possess. Your life is not a movie, with a rerun or rewind at the end; you don't get to do it all again. You are living real time, my friend, so the question is, are you spending the currency of your life in a way that will leave you no regrets at the end of your days?

Back to my office desk: seventeen one pound coins were

what I wanted; each coin would represent a year of my life till I was sixty-five years old. Don't get me wrong, I'm believing for a long and healthy life and have no plans of dying then. Rather these years represented the best ones of my strength and ability. I was forty-eight when I started thinking this way, and I had considered the forty-eight coins spent. Ones wasted, ones well invested, but now, all I could truly plan for were the ones I had left to spend. So I purposed that each year on my birthday, I would move a coin from one pile to another, not out of any morbid fear, but rather out of a desire to inspire me to live fully and get the best value I could out of the ones I had left. At the time of writing this, I have sixteen coins left and one has already moved and started the new pile. There is no regret, however, because when I look back at what I purchased with that coin this past year, I smile and am thankful to God that is was very well spent.

What will you spend the currency of your days on? Things that won't matter? Don't get me wrong, life is a gift and God wants us to enjoy it and live it to the full, especially appreciating things like friends and family; but not at the cost of living selfishly and not for others. In my opinion, the greatest inheritance comes from what we did to improve the lives of other people, especially those who could not help themselves. I have a sneaky feeling that when God sees people living beyond themselves and spending the currency of their lives on behalf of others, it inspires Him to give them a little extra time, wouldn't you?

The people in this Redemption Army are people who have

considered the currency of their days and made a decision to allow them to become God's currency. They have thankfully committed the days of their life to God, to be a currency that He can spend as He desires. They are people that understand that, as the Bible says, their lives are not their own. Our lives in reality are the currency of God already, and we are actually only letting Him use what He already owns.

> Or do you not know that your body is the temple of the Holy Spirit who is in you, whom you have from God, and you are not your own?
>
> **1 Corinthians 6:19**

Remember Jesus led the way in that He was willing to spend the currency of His earthly days on the redemption of humanity. He gladly laid aside His majesty and came to Earth on a mission to lay down His life, the currency of His days, as a ransom price for many. He now calls us to lay down our lives for the benefit others, too.

PEOPLE WHO FEEL POSITIVELY OBLIGED

This army is made up of people who feel obliged. They are motivated by a grace-filled obligation to fulfil a heavenly mandate to impact the lives of others. The dictionary defines the word obligation in a number of ways including: *feeling bound to do something* or *to feel a sense of duty.*

The latter is the one that best describes this obligation

that fuels the heart of a Redemption Army. They feel a sense of duty, a duty or responsibility to pay it forward. By that I mean to now take God's freedom to others. They feel this because once someone came beyond the boundaries of their lives and carried this same freedom to them. Obligation is a word that has had a fair amount of negative press in the modern church over recent years. So-called experts declaring things such as, 'Just be blessed and thankful that people come, don't make them feel obliged.' This is the very type of Christianity that is sinking the church in our generation. Leaders should not desire to raise churches where people are encouraged to sit quietly and be pampered. That results in nothing more than a storage unit for people! Rather, it's time for the church to be mobilised, for us to raise up, equip and release the people. We as church leaders have been guilty of seating people a little bit too comfortably for far too long. There really is an obligation for those who have received redemption from God, a duty to now impact others. Freely we have been given, now freely we should pay it forward.

I believe that there is such a thing as negative obligation in church life, especially when it is fuelled by guilt rather than inspired by desire. However, we cannot throw out the message completely, especially when it comes to being commissioned to reaching the lives of others. Jesus felt obliged to bring redemption to humanity two thousand years ago. He felt obliged to lay down His crown to take up a cross. He felt obliged to leave the courts of heaven to walk dusty streets.

Why did He feel obliged? Because He knew His Father's heart for the humanity He came to redeem. He loved us enough to lay aside His deity so that we could be brought home to the household of His Father. When we consider the brutality of the cross, the scorn and shame He gladly took for us, how can we not feel obliged or have a natural sense of duty towards reaching others and bringing God's redemption to them also?

The Great Commission is an obligation. Let's call it what it is. It's not a suggestion and should never be an omission. It's an obligation to go; go as those who have received His redemption, to the lives of others who have not yet experienced it. This redemptive army is made of people that feel obliged to march, with a divine obligation, not feeling used or abused or hard done by, but privileged and honoured that God would count them worthy to be in His Redemption Army.

PEOPLE WHO HAVE A PASSION TO SEE THEIR SOCIETY REDEEMED

This army of people understands that it is not just individuals and communities that can be redeemed, but also society itself. They understand that it is their duty to actively seek to protect and revive society by defending and making known the knowledge of God in our modern-day world. History has proved time and again that it is the presence of the knowledge of God in any given society that causes that society to remain strong and healthy.

They are a people who are not afraid to stand up for what they believe and know to be true; who purpose to stand

against the strategies that Satan has to pull down everything good, holy and righteous about society. They are like a godly defence wall: they stand to protect society from his eroding waves and subtle schemes.

They are an army of people who have found their voice and refuse to stay silent when things that affect the moral foundations of our society are tampered with by people with an agenda to see anything related to God and His ways removed. This Redemption Army understands that they are God's salt and light in this world, and they refuse to hide their influence or point of view under any basket of embarrassment or apathy.

> 'You are the salt of the earth; but if the salt loses its flavour, how shall it be seasoned? It is then good for nothing but to be thrown out and trampled underfoot by men. You are the light of the world. A city that is set on a hill cannot be hidden. Nor do they light a lamp and put it under a basket, but on a lampstand, and it gives light to all who are in the house. Let your light so shine before men, that they may see your good works and glorify your Father in heaven.'
>
> **Matthew 5:13-16**

They have resolved in their hearts not to be the few good men that do nothing while evil prevails; rather, they speak out and stand up whenever and wherever they see things being tampered with that have formed the very moral stability of society for generations.

The redemption of our post-modern society really is based upon an army of God-lovers who have found their voice, daring to defend the knowledge of God on the face of the earth and not being scared to take a stand when deceived leaders carrying alternative wisdom continually demand the removal of God and His ways.

The church you see remains God's defence against the eroding plans and intentions of an enemy who has always desperately sought for the removal of His ways from the earth. Since the Garden of Eden, this has been the enemy's strategy and greatest desire. Why? Because he knows that it is God's ways lived out in a society that enables it to remain strong, healthy and good. The removal of God and His ways from a society will always lead to moral corruption and a downward spiral in social behaviour, as men do what is right in their own eyes. Over the course of history we have witnessed moments where God's presence was removed, or the knowledge of God watered down, and in every instance society suffered. It has never prospered because, as the self-appointed experts forget, God's principles are the fibre and the building blocks for a healthy society, and are the very foundation for making it solid and secure. The momentary glove puppet who demands the removal of God's ways may change, but the hand within never does. It's the same hand that has had the same agenda from day one – that agenda – to remove the ways of God from the earth. Those who seek to do this often feel that they are radical in their society-shaping

idealism, but in fact they are unknowingly just yielding to the timeless agenda of an anti-Christ spirit, they are just puppets being used and not even realising it.

Think about it, when you take a good sober look at modern-day society today you can see the unrelenting waves of the 'we know better than God' thinking. It constantly beats against the very foundation of our society. It is not a new thing but it is our time to be the wall of defence. God calls us, the church, to actively stand against an ungodly erosion of society in our generation, just as men like William Booth did in his time. William Booth didn't just preach in pulpits and on street corners, he also defended God's ways in the courts of government, especially in regard to people's rights, well-being and the social health of the society he was a part of. He was a reformer, a godly man who brought about the reforming of laws that mistreated people. He had a voice that impacted society itself to be redeemed to godly order and he used that voice to bring change. He spent the currency of his days to see his society reformed and redeemed, rather than only the lives of individuals in it. I believe this Redemption Army is rising up again with people who will actively and unashamedly promote the knowledge of God in their generation; who are not afraid to stand for its redemptive defence.

The bizarre thing to me is that if the people who are so desperate to see God removed could only get a glimpse of how society would actually be if they succeeded, I believe they would instantly turn on their heels and cry out for the reinstitution of God's ways! Let me say once again, a society that has God's principles and values removed from it becomes a place of anarchy and great wickedness; a place where anything goes! Just like it was in the days of Noah before God flooded the earth, a place where sin abounded without any moral conscience or compass. When you read the account of Noah and the genealogy leading up to the flood, it is sobering to think it only took nine generations for the devil to almost totally remove the knowledge of God from the face of the earth. How could that have happened? Simply because people never stood up for or defended it!

Like the seawalls of any coastal town that stand by day and by night relentless resisting the eroding intentions of the battering waves, we, the church, are a godly seawall defence in our generation. A defence that stands for the knowledge of God, that actively seeks the protection and well-being of the society we live in, rather than its destruction, ruin or decay.

Think about it. Have you noticed the effects of the slow but gradual erosion taking place all around you? The Bible (representing God's ways), removed from our courts when law was actually based on it, prayer removed from schools and our armed forces. Just look how well the removal of prayer worked in the American schools – take God out and you will then have to bring metal detectors in to scan the kids for weapons – because without godly principles things always go into chaos.

The rising up of specialised societies like the secular society and atheist movements that actually make it their mandate and purpose to remove the God we know and His ways from every aspect of modern-day society. The atheists now are actually forming their own church, not realising that far from being a church, they are just a group of stubborn, self-willed people who corporately gather around deception instead of acknowledging their Creator. All these misguided folk are operating unknowingly from an ancient anti-Christ spirit. One of their goals was to remove Christ from Christmas. Not realising the stupidity of that pursuit, it's like trying to remove the burger from a beefburger: all you are left with is a bun. No, I'm sorry, but for my family and me, it will never be 'Happy Holidays' or any other nice wintertime festival – it will always be Christmas, with Christ at the very centre of it. Its fundamental purpose being the celebration of the birth of Jesus, God's redeemer sent to seek and save the lost, of which I was one.

Are these people really so blind as to not see the cracks that are appearing in the foundation of our society because of their pursuits? These subtle erosions are causing cracks of perversity, greed, rebellion and dishonour of every kind, just to name a few. They are deluded by the devil and their own foolishness to the long-term effects of their momentary feel-good ideas. Often these changes seem so small or insignificant, like the lowering of ratings on movies, or the permitting of strong language or tasteless controversial scenes on family-time television. They justify doing so with shouts of 'free speech' and 'inclusion'. Yet they do not hear the crumbling of the foundation their pursuits are causing. We need to find our voice and stand for the ways of God that the devil is ever seeking to erode. If we do not speak up and stand up for redemption, these slight changes will keep on taking place because there will be no one to stop them.

Apparently one of the last things some people did on the *Titanic* just before it sank was have a snowball fight. How sad and ironic as, unknowingly, they played and had fun with the very stuff that had just caused the safe platform beneath their feet to be ruined. The snow they used to play and make merry with came from the iceberg that was sinking them. In the same way, these anti-God modern thinkers do not realise that like those people playing with snowballs, they are unknowingly playing with things that have the potential to sink society. If they are allowed to keep removing God and His ways from everything without any remorse, then, like the *Titanic*, everything good about society will sink. It will be too late for us to think again concerning things now lost or ruined. Sadly, many in the church are remarkably like another group on the *Titanic* that night. These people were actually asleep and slept through most of the early stages of what was happening, blissfully unaware as they slept on, not realising that what they had put their confidence in was now damaged and sinking. The Bible speaks so relevantly to these 'sleeping saints' when it says:

Arise, shine, for your light has come, and the glory of

the Lord rises upon you. See, darkness covers the earth and thick darkness is over the peoples, but the Lord rises upon you and his glory appears over you.

Isaiah 60:1-2 (NIV)

We, my friends, are to be that needed seawall, we are to be the salt and light of God's kingdom in this world that contends for the retaining of His ways in society. Whether in the classrooms of education or corridors of local government, we must find our voice, we must stand up, we must speak. God is not calling us to physically fight, but He is calling us to warfare. Our warfare is to stand for His knowledge and ways in our generation, and to pull down every other knowledge or high thing that tries to exalt itself above the knowledge of God.

For the weapons of our warfare are not carnal but mighty in God for pulling down strongholds, casting down arguments and every high thing that exalts itself against the knowledge of God, bringing every thought into captivity to the obedience of Christ.

2 Corinthians 10:4-5

It is vital that we understand that when God's knowledge and ways are removed, then things go into chaos and destruction. Whether in the life of an individual, a community or society, when God's wisdom and ways are removed, things implode and disintegrate. In a healthy society, God's ways are the very fibre of the fabric of everything people

love and hold dear. The removal of God and His ways can only create destruction as it says in Hosea 4:6, even God's people are destroyed through lack of His knowledge.

PASS IT ON, PASS IT DOWN

As well as being people who choose to stand for His knowledge, let's also purpose to be those who pass it on to those around us and pass it down to those who follow us. One of the things I love about early Jewish culture is the way that parents handed down the ways of God from one generation to another. Parents and grandparents would hand down the knowledge of God to their children and grand-children. This is how the understanding of who God was to the Jews survived and thrived through so many thousands of years, even during great and terrible persecution. As Christians, we also have a responsibility to pass on the knowledge of God to others. That's discipleship in its purest form. We need to especially pass it down to our children. Parents, it is your responsibility to let your children know what you've learned about God and His ways so they can love and know Him like you have. Don't stay quiet; start by putting the Bible again on the breakfast table, and begin to teach your kids the ways of God. Don't just leave it to the Sunday school teachers – it's not only their job – it's yours.

We are those who seek the redemption of our society by standing for and promoting the knowledge of God in it; we will not stay quiet, we will not sit down, we will not watch

on as people try to remove things that should never be removed or tampered with.

CONCLUSION

This Redemption Army is made up of people who feel obliged, who have considered the currency of their days and purposed to not stay quiet but to take a stand for the God they adore. They have purposed in their hearts to let God use their life to make a difference in the lives of others, and to be a difference for God in the society He has entrusted them to be a part of. I suppose that only leaves one last question. How about you, will you be a part of this Redemption Army?

IAMREDEMP†ION.org STORIES

Fight for healthy body

We'd been praying for six years for a new kidney, and in mid-January I was called into Queen Alexandria Hospital, Portsmouth, as I was to receive the long-awaited kidney. From the moment I was returned to the ward the doctors were amazed at the performance of the kidney, and I even got to go home early.

But two months later I was rushed back in for a bowel obstruction and a perforated bowel. I was poisoning myself from the inside. Several operations later, and three visits to ICU, I felt the prayers again, and I had the same team as for my kidney operation looking after me. I even had nurses from my church watching over me! My three children were amazing during that whole time – they where called in six times to say goodbye, but God's resurrection power saved me each time. I cried out to God on at least three occasions to take me home to heaven, and then the next day I would be sitting up and feel whole again.

Throughout this time the kidney kept steady. My memory is vague about the whole time, but I remember the sense of prayers being lifted up for me, and the support of family and my church pastors. Recovery is still on-going, but I have already exceeded the time-plan of the medical team

Paul

IAMREDEMP†ION
Manifesto

see an army of everyday people rising up who will passionately carry and make known through word and action the redemptive heart of God in our generation, a people who:

† Represent different generations, cultures and walks of life, who know their lives have been redeemed – "purchased back to God and wholeness" – through the love and power of the living God. (Revelation 5:9)

† Are non-religious and marked by "mercy and grace", believing that Jesus' one-time, sacrificial act of giving His life on the cross paid the bill for their freedom – a bill that they could never pay themselves, a bill that was not just about their freedom but that of all humanity. (Ephesians 2:8)

† Know that God can change the storyline of a person's life and cause his or her story to have a fresh chapter or a better ending, no matter who they are; who believe that no person is unreachable, or any situation too impossible that God cannot turn it around. (John 10:10)

† Passionately believe that the Father heart of God is one of redemption and reconciliation; that it is His will and desire that none should perish in life or eternity, and have made "That none would perish" their battle cry. (2 Peter 3:9)

† Are unashamed concerning the Gospel and will not stay silent about what God has done in their life, or settle for hiding behind rocks of insecurity, fear or excuse, but will be a part of a redeemed people who "say so" about what God has done in their life as God gives them opportunity. (Romans 1:16, Psalm 107:2)

† Know, like the liberated donkey in Luke 19, that their lives have been freed by God to be used by God; a people who daily purpose to carry the redemptive heart of God, who gladly bear their backs to be a willing vehicle for Him, ready and privileged to take Him wherever, and to whomever, He wants to go. (Luke 10:28-31)

† Are never "too busy" to allow their lives to be God's "redemptive interruptions" in the lives of others, so that those lives can also be re-routed to a better destination and future; a people that do not mind God spending the currency of their life on His redemptive plans for others. (2 Corinthians 12:15)

† Are not afraid to lay down their lives to be "redemptive pathways" that God can use between Himself and Man, so that others can have a clear pathway to knowing Him and experiencing the life change He offers. (1 John 3:16, John 15:13)

† Do not carry or represent a message of judgement, guilt or fear that repels people from God, but rather one of love, grace and mercy that draws a person to Him. (John 3:16-17)

† Are God's modern-day Samaritans, that don't cross the road when they see others in need but rather step into real-life situations to see the lives of others, even those they don't know, redeemed and made better. (Luke 10: 25-37)

† Know they are called and commissioned to be God's "ambassadors" on the earth, delivering to others they meet in their daily life the invitation of God to be reconciled to back to Him. (2 Corinthians 5:18-20)

† Have realised the God has called and empowered them to not just carry His redemptive heart but also to be His arms and feet in people's needs and situations. (Acts 1:8)

† See people and communities, that others may walk past or have given up on, through God's eyes of redemptive intention; they simply cannot, and refuse to, give up on what God has not given up on.

† No longer find contentment just sitting or being 'stored' in the churches they attend, but want to be trained and mobilised by their church to carry redemption to the lives of others. (Ephesians 4: 11-13)

† Put their time and money where their mouth is, fully aware that redemption always has a cost, just as it cost God His only beloved Son to redeem humanity; who know there will always be a bill in bringing God's redemption (wholeness) to the lives of others – whether it is time, money or sacrifice, they are willing to pay the bill and cover the cost to see others experience God's freedom. (1 Peter 1:18-19)

† Believe that the Great Commission given by Jesus in the 1st century is still their commission in the 21st Century; they refuse to treat it like a suggestion and will never allow it to be an omission; the call to "Go" remains the Great Commission upon their lives that drives and motivates them to reach and make a difference for Jesus in the lives of others today. (Matthew 28:18-19)

IAMREDEMP†ION
The Fund

Why not partner with us as we purpose to be IAMREDEMPTION in the lives of others? We are constantly working to bring redemption to people and communities and have many ongoing projects, as well as some we are dreaming of doing. Want to partner with us?

Rebuilding homes in the village of St Andréas, in the Philippines, where previously there stood wooden shacks that were completely washed away in the typhoon of December 2013.

We have a number of projects on the go at any one time, everything from providing safe housing and refuge so that vulnerable girls are safe, to building homes in rural villages for those made homeless by extreme weather conditions. Other projects involve creating industry in rural villages so that communities can establish a sustainable economy and not be

Through the iamredemption fund, a village in the Philippines has established a new industry to help revitalise their economy during the months where there is no harvest or crop to manage.

dependant on others. We help individuals in different parts of the world who, for one reason or another, are struggling, in danger, or needing protection or just a helping hand. This fund enables those who to desire to partner with us enabling us to take on projects that would be to big for us to do alone – you are welcome to join us.

Contact us at: info@iamredemption.org
or send donations to:
IAMREDEMPTION
83-87 Kingston Road
Portsmouth,
Hants,
PO2 7DX
UK

Prayer

I hope you enjoyed this book and that is has been both a blessing and a challenge to your life and walk with God. Maybe you just got hold of it and are looking through before starting. Long ago, I made the decision never to take for granted that everyone has prayed a prayer to receive Jesus as their Lord, so am including that as the finale to this book. If you have never asked Jesus into your life and would like to do that now, it's so easy. Just pray this simple prayer:

> Dear Lord Jesus, thank You for dying on the cross for me. I believe that You gave Your life so that I could have life. When You died on the cross, You died as an innocent man who had done nothing wrong. You were paying for my sins and the debt I could never pay. I believe in You, Jesus, and receive the brand new life and fresh start that the Bible promises that I can have. Thank You for my sins forgiven, for the righteousness that comes to me as a gift from You, for hope and love beyond what I have known and the assurance of eternal life that is now mine. Amen.

Good next moves are to get yourself a Bible that is easy to

understand and begin to read. Maybe start in John so you can discover all about Jesus for yourself. Start to pray – prayer is simply talking to God – and, finally, find a church that's alive and get your life planted in it. These simple ingredients will cause your relationship with God to grow.

Why not email me and let me know if you did that so I can rejoice with you? Tell me about your redemption story.

Andy Elmes, response@greatbiglife.co.uk

Further Information

For further information about the author of this book, or to order more copies, please contact:

Great Big Life Publishing
Empower Centre
83-87 Kingston Road
Portsmouth
Hants
PO2 7DX
UK

info@greatbiglifepublishing.com
www.greatbiglifepublishing.com
@GBLPublishing

Are you an Author?

Do you have a word from God on your heart that you're looking to get published to a wider audience? We're looking for manuscripts that identify with our own vision of bringing life-giving and relevant messages to Body of Christ. Send yours for review towards possible publication to:

Great Big Life Publishing
Empower Centre
83-87 Kingston Road
Portsmouth
Hants
PO2 7DX
UK

or, email us at info@greatbiglifepublishing.com

Sign up to receive fresh, daily devotionals via email:
www.breakfastofchampions.co.uk

breakfast of
CHAMPIONS

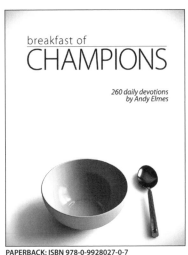

PAPERBACK: ISBN 978-0-9928027-0-7
EBOOK: ISBN 978-0-9928027-1-4

260 daily devotions
by Andy Elmes

Breakfast of Champions is a mid-week devotional written with the purpose of inspiring you to live the most effective, influential, God-filled life you can. Packed with wisdom and tips taken from his own colourful walk with God, Andy will inspire and challenge you to daily "run your best race". This devotional, served up alongside your Bible each day, will give your spirit the nutrition and fibre it needs to grow strong and healthy. God's Word truly is the breakfast of Champions!

WHAT ARE THEY SAYING?

"Andy Elmes lives life to the full with contagious joy, constantly extending the kingdom of God. He communicates with one person as though he/she is the most important person on earth. A very engaging and humorous preacher, he hits the mark every time and large crowds of people remember his messages for years. Andy is a great leader who is impacting thousands of lives around the world."

Ashley Schmierer, International President, Christian Outreach Centre global movement of churches

"It's been my privilege to be a friend of Andy's for several years now and I have come to know and value his visionary and inspirational leadership. Andy has a wealth of experience to offer in so many ways and I particularly value his regular 'devotionals' which, like me, so many have found to be very relevant and helpful in their daily lives. I'm sure this book will bring prosperity and success to all who read it. Well done, Andy."

Linvoy Primus, professional footballer and co-founder of Faith & Football

Available from
Great Big Life Publishing
greatbiglifepublishing.com • @GBLPublishing

It's time for the 21st century church to return to a 1st century vision

Two thousand years ago, when Jesus declared that He would build His Church, He rolled out a blueprint of what the Church was meant to be – relevant and effective through all generations. We now find ourselves in the 21st century, and we need to ask ourselves, "When we roll out the blueprint we currently have for 'building the Church', does it look the same as His? Are we building the Church Jesus wants built?"

In this compelling book, Andy Elmes, speaking from years of experience as a church leader, evangelist, and leadership coach, sends out a passionate call to the modern-day Church to return to "the blueprint" of God, building Church once again according to the pattern handed down to us by the architect, Jesus.

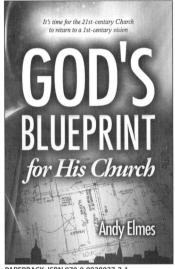

PAPERBACK: ISBN 978-0-9928027-2-1
EBOOK: ISBN 978-0-9928027-3-8

Andy challenges us to reconsider the importance of topics like:
- The Great Commission – is Church to be seeker-friendly, mission-minded, or both?
- Discipleship – what place should it have in modern church?
- The power of God – are we building safe churches or supernatural ones?

Together we will revisit these and other subjects to see how today's Church lines up with God's original plans and intentions for His House. Is it time for the 21st century Church to return to a 1st century vision? And how do we do that both effectively and relevantly in our generation?

Available from
Great Big Life Publishing
greatbiglifepublishing.com • @GBLPublishing

How far would you go
to refresh your leader?

'If truth be told, most senior pastors would love to write a book for their leadership teams called *How I Would Serve Me If I Was You*. The reality is most won't, yet what is on their heart needs to be heard. So I dared to write it for them!'

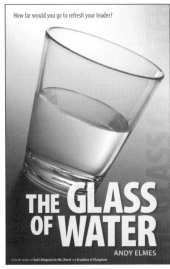

In this sometimes brutally honest book, Andy shares insights on what it is like to be a senior leader of a church, looking with great transparency at the natural and spiritual pressures facing the leader who has decided to do something for God. He also asks the question, 'Where are the mighty men?' – those men and women whom God desires to surround the leader with. He asks a number of very honest questions:

- What do mighty men look like and what do they do?
- What are the hallmarks and characteristics of a mighty man?
- What does the leader need their team to do for them?
- What have 'holding up Moses' arms' and 'being an armour bearer' got to do with us in the 21st century?

PAPERBACK: ISBN 978-1-4823513-1-6

This book is written to be intentionally provocative. You will journey into the often unseen world of the leader God has given you, seeing things you never knew and that they would never tell you, and discovering how challenging the calling they received can sometimes be.

'My desire in writing this book is to stop pastors quitting by initiating vital conversations. I want to provoke the mighty men and women that are out there to have a greater awareness concerning the leader God has given them; to stand up and step up to a new level; to be what they should be so that the leader and their family can be all that God has commissioned them to be.' *Andy Elmes*

Take this thought-provoking journey to discover what a difference a simple glass of water can really make.

Available from
Great Big Life Publishing
greatbiglifepublishing.com • @GBLPublishing